I'm not OK and you're not OK either

The Neurotic's Handbook

Susan F. Young

BLOOMSBURY

For
Alexa de Ferranti
with thanks

First published in Great Britain 1991

Copyright © 1991 by Susan F. Young

This paperback edition published 1991

The moral right of the author has been asserted

Bloomsbury Publishing Ltd, 2 Soho Square, London W1V 5DE

A CIP catalogue record for this book
is available from the British Library

ISBN 0 7475 0887 9

Typeset by Rowland Phototypesetting Ltd, Bury St Edmunds, Suffolk
Printed by Cox & Wyman Ltd, Reading, Berks.

CONTENTS

v

INTRODUCTION

Somewhere on this planet there are perfect people. People who are completely sane, well-balanced and generally untroubled by the fears, insecurities and personal eccentricities that afflict everyone else. We will call these people the Un-neurotic.

Un-neurotics have calmly and methodically read every self-help book on the market. They've spent more time in analysis than Woody Allen. They've improved their memories, their language skills, their cooking and their personal relationships. They are not afraid of dogs, spiders, the drinking water, electricity, or riding in lifts. They get along well with machines, neighbours, and people in positions of authority. They never abuse power. They like themselves – all the time. They're happy with their bodies and the way they look. They don't mind getting old. An Un-neurotic would never get halfway to work and then get off the bus and go all the way back home because she'd discovered a run in her tights. An Un-neurotic would never comb eight strands of hair across his forehead so no one would know he was going bald. Likewise, the homes of Un-neurotics are always clean and tidy and in good repair. They don't forget to have the hot water taps fixed for a year-and-a-half. They don't learn to live with that missing step. You can open any drawer and cupboard without the possibility of an avalanche or explosion. These people never argue with their parents, yell at their children, or cry in public. Un-neurotics are never bossy or aggressive. They don't nag. They never say, 'Do you have the keys? Are you sure you have the keys? You have the keys, don't you? Darling, where did you put the keys?' over and over and over again. On the other hand, Un-neurotics never let people take advantage of them or push them around, either. The

Un-neurotics get plenty of sleep, good food and exercise. They know how to take a joke. These people do nothing to excess. No, *nothing*. 'Yuk,' these people say. 'Why would anyone want to eat an entire packet of chocolate biscuits in one sitting?' 'Ick,' they further say, 'why would anyone want to drink so much that he winds up sleeping in the car on someone else's front lawn?'

Un-neurotics make good mates, great guests, wonderful politicians, policemen and salespeople, and perfect siblings, children, coworkers, bosses and business associates. They have no bad habits, no weakness, no little fetishes. 'Why would anyone bite their nails?' queries the Un-neurotic. 'Why would anyone need to check his horoscope every day?' The Un-neurotic shakes his head, baffled. 'Why would an intelligent, ordinary person refuse to leave the house without his lucky charm?' They are always methodical and logical. Reasonable, even. Guilt? These people know nothing of guilt. Inferiority complex? They think it's a cheaply-made shopping development. Overcompensation? They think overcompensation is what happens when the insurance company pays you too much. Harbour petty jealousies, hurts, or desires for revenge? You must be joking. An Un-neurotic doesn't hate Sharon Simpson for twenty years because when they were at school together Sharon Simpson always did better than she did in English. An Un-neurotic doesn't saw the heels from his wife's shoes because she wants a trial separation.

'You mean they don't break out in a rash in crowded superstores?'

No, they don't. They don't even start major family arguments in them.

'They don't refuse to tell their mother anything about their lives, and then yell at her because she never asks them about themselves?'

It wouldn't cross their minds.

'They can go out on a first date without spending four hours getting ready and ending up wearing the first thing they tried on?'

They do it all the time.

'And what about sex?'

What about it? They do that all the time, too. *And* they never worry about not getting it up, not getting it in, or falling asleep before it's all over.

'Are you expecting us to believe that there are people in the civilized world who are never so terrified of opening a bill or a notice from the tax office that they put it in a drawer and forget about it until the phone's turned off or the bailiffs arrive?'

Yes, I am. There really are people who open every piece of correspondence they receive immediately and pay all accounts promptly.

'They never listen in on the answering machine to see who's calling?'

Wouldn't dream of it. They don't even assume that that's what everyone else is doing to them.

'Wow. That's incredible. Perfect, completely sane and rational human beings. Where can I meet them?'

Well, that can be a little difficult.

'Difficult? Really? And why is that?'

Because there are only three of them.

'Three of them? In the entire world?'

Yes, three. Precisely three. In the entire world.

'Including Antarctica?'

We can't count animals or flightless birds.

'Three Un-neurotic people on the planet Earth!' you exclaim, shaking your head. 'That seems just incredible, considering The Renaissance, The Age of Reason, Sigmund Freud and executive toys!'

Personally, I'm surprised there are so many.

WHY AM I SO STUPID/UGLY/ INADEQUATE . . . ?

Body Obsession

Everyone is concerned with his or her body. After all, it's *there*, isn't it? You can't ever put it away and forget about it. Some people, however, have turned their concern into something else. No, we're not talking about aerobics, macrobiotics or environmentally friendly deodorants; we're talking here about obsession.

• You are concerned about your weight. Your best friend, in your opinion ill-advisedly travelling through South America, is arrested as a CIA agent and put into a cell so deep they have to pump air into it. When, after several weeks, your friend is released and sent home, the first thing you say to her is: 'I don't know what you're complaining about, you must have lost at least two stone.'

• You like to take care of your teeth. You carry a toothbrush with you at all times. You spend ten minutes every morning studying your gums. While watching television, a time when most people eat snack foods or think about sewing that button on their shirts, you floss your teeth.

• You keep your make-up in a dresser drawer. The drawer is full.

• The last person to see your naked feet was your mother, when you were six.

• Where another person might say, 'Um, feta cheese omelette, buttered toast and sausage', you would say either, 'There goes my bikini' or 'Ugh! Suicide by cholesterol'.

• You would sleep on a brick if you thought it would do something for your chin. The reason you know it won't do anything for your chin is because you have, in the past, slept on a brick.

• You think Michael Jackson has the right idea.

• When your beloved was having that affair that time, the only thought in your head was, 'Please, lord, don't let her be thin'.

• You can't eat in Japanese restaurants because they give you those hot towels to rub on your face, and if you rub a hot towel on your face your make-up comes off. You could, of course, *not* rub the towel on your face, but then your dinner companion might ask why you

3

weren't, and you might have to explain about the make-up. You don't want anyone to know about the make-up.

- You haven't bought any new clothes in years, because you can't face those open changing-rooms.
- There is no bulb in your house over forty watts.
- Not a day goes by that you don't think about your nose.
- Even your best friend thinks that you can't swim, because you refuse to go within ten miles of a beach. In fact, you swim very well. You even enjoy swimming. But you refuse to sport swimwear in public. Not with your bum/hairy body/flat chest/upper arms.
- Eventually, on holiday in Samoa, which is little more than a beach if you get right down to it, you are dragged to the beach. You swim in a T-shirt and cut-offs.
- On your fortieth birthday, you hung a black cloth over every reflective surface in the house.
- It takes you three hours before you can leave the house in the morning.
- You rarely manage to leave the house in the morning.
- You brush your hair more than twice a day.
- You cut yourself out of group photographs.
- You cut yourself out of photographs that are just of you and a tree.
- You can't pass a shop window without looking at yourself.
- You know exactly what you look like from the back.
- If anyone, in passing, says something like, 'Doesn't Ronald have nice teeth/hair/a good body/terrific skin?' you immediately assume that they are saying that you don't.
- Every time you see a photograph of yourself you cry.
- You would rather walk off a cliff than wear glasses.
- You put on your new glasses to show your friends. 'Well,' you say, 'what do you think?' Your friends say, 'They're very large,' and 'I dig that green.' You instantly whip off the glasses and shout as you storm from the room, 'Oh, I see, you think I look ridiculous!'
- Your first thought when meeting someone new is, 'Is s/he less attractive than I am?'
- The amount of money you spend every year on skin creams, moisturizers, etc., would feed a family of four for a year.
- You turned down a date with Cher, because you were afraid that if the evening went well there might be a point in the relationship where

you would be expected to take off your shirt. You take off your shirt for no one.

● At the public swimming pool, you take your shower with your shirt on.

● You use an anti-perspirant, a deodorant, a body mousse, and a scent. *And* you bathe or shower more than once a day.

● You weigh yourself daily.

● You not only weigh yourself, you know at exactly what time to weigh yourself so you'll be at your optimum weight.

Ageing

Ageing is one of those things, like dying, that everyone does but no one wants to. And the more you don't want to, the more neurotic about it you tend to become.

When you're a child and you ask your mother how old she is, your mother says, 'Twenty-nine.'

Your mother is twenty-nine for a good twelve years before you realize that she isn't telling you the truth. 'Mum,' you say, 'you can't be twenty-nine. If you're twenty-nine then you must have been seventeen when you had me, but you didn't meet Dad till you were twenty-one.'

Your mother dives into the refrigerator for something. 'Twenty-nine plus,' she mutters.

'Plus what?' you innocently ask.

'Plus none of your business,' snaps your mother. 'Now go and play in your room or you'll find yourself in some real trouble.'

You find this all pretty strange. Why should your mother be so touchy about her age? It's no big deal. After all, you've never had trouble admitting to being twelve, have you?

Time passes.

When you're twenty, and have begun to understand that your mother is not the only person in the world who has either forgotten the year of her birth or turns nasty when pushed about it, you say, 'I don't know why people get hung up on age. It's not how old you are that counts, it's how old you feel.' You feel pretty young. Young enough to make an announcement. 'I will never be neurotic about my age,' you announce on several occasions. 'Absolutely never. I swear it.'

More time passes.

You hit thirty. For many people, hitting thirty is like running into a brick wall. You knew the wall was there all the time, right ahead of you, but somehow it never occurred to you that you were going to hit it. Everyone else, yes; but not you. But then comes the day that you notice that first grey hair. You let out an anguished cry. 'Don't panic,' you say to the ashen face in the mirror. 'It may not be anything. It may just be the light.' It isn't just the light. It isn't even just a grey hair. It's indisputable proof that you're getting old. You pull it out.

You pull out the next twenty grey hairs as well. By the time you've staggered through the rubble of this particular brick wall you are spending the Friday night you used to spend dancing till dawn secretly dying your hair and rubbing anti-ageing creams into your face.

Time slogs on.

The anti-ageing creams aren't working. You're ageing. Lines are appearing on your once smooth skin. Your muscles are sagging. Your chin begins to drop. Something awful is happening to your neck. Something worse is happening to you. Forty. When you were twenty, thirty seemed a long way away – and now it seems a long way away again. Every time you look in the mirror you cry out in alarm. Who is that staring back at you? That can't be *you*! You look like your father. 'This must be a dream,' you say to the stranger in the mirror. 'I never looked like my father before. I was always cute and young, and he was always over the hill.' You rub your eyes. Behind the reflection in the bathroom mirror you can see a hill, shrinking in the distance. Your mature and sensible response to this is to put forty-watt bulbs in the bathroom and avoid daylight.

You lose your birth certificate. 'How could you have lost your birth certificate?' your wife wants to know. 'It was right in the box with the others.' You blame her.

When filling out forms you leave Date of Birth blank, hoping no one will notice. You make your children call you by your first name.

Depressed by monitoring your own ageing process, you start paying scrupulous attention to how well your friends are ageing. Do they have more grey hairs than you do? Do they have less hair? Have they already lost their chins? Their teeth? Their ability to sprint for a bus? Are those varicose veins or patterned tights? While pretending to be listening closely to Rachel's story about finding the frozen spinach in the umbrella stand, you are, in fact, closely studying her face for lines and creases that your face doesn't have (or, to be more exact, that you don't think your face has, since you can't possibly know, because you never look at your face in anything but shadow). You lie awake at night, listening to your skin wrinkle. You storm out of the chemist's because the sales assistant calls you 'Madam'.

You leave your wife of twenty-five years and begin to date women who are too young for you. When your friends tease you about it ('Heh, heh, George, but what does *she* do for sex'), you convince yourself that they're jealous. 'Mike wishes he could go out with a girl younger than his daughter, that's what the problem is,' you say. You take to playing rugby on Saturday afternoons, just like you did when you were twelve; and to taking your girlfriend to discos on Saturday nights, just like you never did in your life.

Whenever someone asks you how old you are you change the subject quickly, or say, 'Twenty-nine plus,' as though it's a joke.

Dressing

Alicia Whitman-Smythe is marrying Justin Bingley-Browne, and you're invited! Lucky you! The bride will be in white satin with a handmade lace train and veil. The bridesmaids will be wearing floor-length maroon dresses with beaded sleeves. The groom will be in a rented tuxedo. What will you be in?

You put the invitation to the Whitman-Smythe–Bingley-Browne wedding on the coffee table and you march into your bedroom. You open the wardrobe. You start removing outfits, one by one. You will not be wearing the blue linen suit, it's too dull. You will not be wearing the pink cocktail dress. It's too dated. Ditto the yellow silk sheath and the white thing with the flared skirt. Red is not the colour for a wedding like this, and your royal-blue dress isn't nearly formal enough. The crushed velvet gown is formal enough, but Alicia has seen it before. And you wore the taffeta to the last wedding you went to. You could wear a suit, of course, but your best suit is black. You can't wear a black suit to a wedding like this. Everyone will think you're with the caterers.

You collapse on the floor beside the hillock of clothes you've removed from your wardrobe. You will be in nothing for the

Whitman-Smythe–Bingley-Browne wedding, that's what you'll be in.

You pull yourself together. You own enough dresses to clothe half of Guatemala, there must be something in there suitable for this affair.

Every night for two weeks you stand at your wardrobe and sigh. The chartreuse? The burgundy? That navy job? No. No. No. Every night for two weeks you collapse into bed with a crashing headache. You dream about clothes. You're at Alicia's wedding, and everyone looks stunningly wonderful but you. You're wearing an old pair of jeans and a Rolling Stones sweatshirt. You are not mistaken for one of the caterers. You're mistaken for one of the groundskeepers. At work, you're distracted. Your secretary asks you a question. 'Where did you want me to file this?' she asks. And you say, 'What about basic black. That's too low-key, isn't it? Even if I rented a diamond necklace to set it off?'

In the end, you give in and go shopping. The first day you go shopping you go alone. You cry in the changing-room because it is impossible for you to tell whether the salmon is too extravagant or the green too green. The second day you take your mother with you. You and your mother have a fight because she would never wear anything with crinolines at your age. You leave her crying in the changing-room. The third day you go shopping, you take your best friend. She buys herself a suit, a cocktail dress, and a hat. You storm out of the store while she is paying for the hat; let her walk home, the cow. 'Why are you mad at *me*?' she calls after you. 'You know why!' you shout back.

You finally find a dress you like. It's very similar to at least four other dresses already in your wardrobe, but of course the colour's different and no one has ever seen this dress before. Then too, you have shoes to go with the other four dresses, but not with this one. And stockings. And a hat.

Unseasonably – and uncooperatively – it snows the day of the Whitman-Smythe–Bingley-Browne wedding. You weren't counting on this. You have to wear your mac because your winter coat's in storage and there isn't time to rush out and buy another one. Everyone thinks you're with the limousine service.

The Vanity, Vanity, All Is Vanity Quiz

Although we all know that beauty is unimportant compared to so many other things and that Marilyn Monroe was never really happy, we all still get a little defensive when it comes to our looks. A little touchy. A little vain. We may know that we're short, but we don't particularly want anyone else to know. It may not have escaped our attention that our nose is a little on the large size, but that doesn't stop us from unceremoniously stomping out of the room when someone points it out in public. In fact, it is probably fair to say that more people are neurotic about their looks than any other single thing. Here's a little quiz to see how comfortable you are with your physical appearance. I have created some hypothetical situations, the sort of situations that anyone might find her- or himself in from time to time. Choose the answer which best describes how you would respond to each hypothetical situation.

1. You have a date. It's with someone you met at a party who is so intelligent, attractive, witty and wonderful that when this person rang up for the date you were half-tempted to say, 'Are you sure you've got the right number?' The problem is, you also have a spot. It's the first thing you see when you dare to look in the mirror that morning. You wince, but decide to ignore it. If you ignore it, you hope, it will simply go away. The spot does not go away. All morning you poke and prod at it, and all morning it not only doesn't vanish, it throbs and grows. By lunch time it is the size of a walnut and the colour of a stop sign. 'Don't be silly,' your best friend at work reassures you, 'you can hardly notice it.' Everyone notices it. As you walk down the street, small children nudge each other, point and giggle. Adults avert their eyes in horror. Adolescents gape. As you pass the bus stop, you overhear two women talking. 'Now that's what I call big,' says the one. 'Well, you couldn't miss that on a dark night if it was foggy and you were blindfolded, could you?' says the other. There is no doubt in your mind that they are talking about your spot. You reach your front door and race into the bathroom. You heave yourself on to the sink to get close to the

mirror. You scream. If the spot were on your nose, and not on your chin, they'd be calling you Rudolph. You cannot go on a date looking like this. 'Don't panic!' shouts a little voice in your head. 'Put a plaster on it and say that you were in an accident.' You have to make a pretty snap decision here. If you're not going on this date, you're going to have to cancel it before the appointed time of your meeting. If you are going, you only have two hours left in which to get ready. You

a. put on the plaster and spend a great deal of the evening recounting the accident.
b. get your best friend to call up and say that you have the flu.
c. put on the plaster, take off the plaster, put on the plaster, take off the plaster, put on the plaster, go to the restaurant, walk past the restaurant, go back to the restaurant, go back home and take the phone off the hook.
d. get so involved trying to find something to wear on this date that you completely forget about putting on the plaster. You arrive at the restaurant twenty minutes late. The first thing your date says is, 'Good Lord! That's some beacon you've got on your chin!' Without a word, you march into the restroom and lock yourself in a corner stall. Forever.

2. You have been asked to give a speech. A combination of hypnosis, alcohol, tranquillizers, herbs, and astrological reassurance can help you overcome your fear of public speaking, but that is not your biggest fear. Your biggest fear is
a. that someone might notice that you're going bald.
b. that someone might notice that your eyes are too close together.
c. that someone might notice that you have a fat bum.
d. that someone might notice that one of your ears is larger than the other.
e. all of the above.

3. In order to disguise the fact that you're going bald you
a. grow your hair long on one side and comb it over the middle.
b. always wear a hat or scarf. Always.
c. never comb the hair you do have.
d. buy a wig. Only you're afraid that if you wear the wig in

public everyone will think you're going bald, so you only wear it in the house.

4. In order to disguise the fact that your bum is fat you
   a. wear tents.
   b. are always the last to leave the room.
   c. always stand with your back to the wall.
   d. never take your coat off till you know somebody very well.
   e. never stand up.

5. With you, it's not your hair, your bum, your eyes, or your ears that are the problem. It's your teeth. To disguise the fact that when the million-dollar smiles were being handed out you were at the back of the queue, worrying about whether your knees weren't a little too knobbly, you
   a. never smile.
   b. have learned to talk, sing and laugh with your mouth closed so well that you are much in demand as a ventriloquist at children's parties.
   c. have every tooth in your head taken out and replaced with perfect teeth that disprove the saying that man can't improve on nature. He can, and he can make it stain-resistant and chip-proof, too. The unfortunate thing is, however, that your teeth are now too good for your face. Anyone seeing those teeth would know they couldn't possibly belong to you. This means that although you can smile now, you can only do so after dark so no one really notices.
   d. are about to have every tooth in your head replaced with something better, and then have your nose reshaped, your bags removed, your skin planed, your chin tucked and the fat sucked from your hips so that everything matches, when it occurs to you that if you do that and your popularity rating doesn't soar, you won't be able to blame it on the fact that no one would ever ask you to be in a commercial for toothpaste.

6. You are walking down the street one day, thinking the thoughts that one does think when walking down the street: did George in the office *really* mean what he said about my presentation, or was he just being kind; was he not being kind but patronizing instead; is he sneaking behind my back to get that promotion;

was that *really* a wrong number last night or was it someone wanting to see if I was in; did I turn off the iron; did I lock all the doors; do I have my keys; whose keys do I have? It is just as you are about to pass a rather smallish man in a brown bowler that this person, a stranger, stops dead only inches from you. You think this is bloody peculiar so you walk on. 'Oi!' calls the stranger. 'Don't you say hello?' The voice is very familiar. You stop and turn and peer into the stranger's face. It is not a smallish man in a brown bowler after all. It is your cousin Lucy in a green beret. 'Arabella,' says Lucy. 'Do you need glasses?' You say

a. 'No.'

b. 'Glasses? What makes you say that?'

c. 'Actually, I've got my contacts in but they irritate my eyes so much that it's a little hard for me to see.'

d. 'Oh, silly, I knew it was you, Lucy. You never could take a joke, could you?'

Dating

My own mother always taught me that most men are crazy. 'It goes without saying,' said my mother. 'Look at all they're responsible for. War. Politics. Torture. Rape. Automatic car washes. The atomic bomb. Advertising. Shopping precincts. Nipple tassles. *Trivial Pursuit* . . .' The list, we have always agreed, is pretty endless. Not that my mother really blamed them, you understand. 'They probably can't help it,' said my mother. 'After all, men are under an enormous amount of pressure from an early age.'

'You mean like being macho and strong and not vomiting if somebody throws a dead mouse at you?'

'That, too,' said my mother. 'But I was thinking more of having to ask girls out on dates.'

Well, better them than I, that's all I can say.

Will's First Date

All of Will's friends have begun to date. The boys he used to go to the cinema with on a Friday night and throw popcorn at are now going with girls. One of the boys he plays football with has taken a girl's bra off. Even Will's best friend has had a date. There's nothing for it, he's going to have to ask someone to the school dance.

Who?

He can't ask the girl he'd like to ask, Tanya Marlow, because every boy in Will's year has a crush on Tanya, and she knows it. If he asks Tanya she'll laugh in his face.

He could ask Linda Peel, because he knows from several boys who know girls who know Linda that Linda has a crush on Will. So the chances are good that she'd say yes. But none of the other boys think that Linda is pretty. She is pretty, but none of the other boys think so because she doesn't have long hair and giggle a lot. He can't ask out a girl none of the other boys consider pretty. They'll think he asked her because his mother made him or something. Or because he knew she wouldn't dare turn him down.

He can, however, ask Suzanne Widme. Suzanne is not pretty, but she has long hair and she giggles a lot, so all the boys think she's all right. But she's not so all right that she'd rather go grocery shopping with her mother than to the dance with him.

How?

His mother says that all he has to do is pick up the telephone and ring Suzanne's number. When she comes to the phone, he should say, 'Hello, Suzanne, this is Will. Would you like to go to the dance with me?' His mother says it's easy.

Will locks himself in the bathroom and spends an hour or so rehearsing this speech. Finally, having committed it pretty much to memory, he approaches the telephone. Looking just a little to the left, he sees his entire family, sitting in the sitting-room, watching television. He hadn't counted on this. There is no way he can ask Suzanne Widme to the dance with his entire family listening to him. He asks them if they could please leave the room for a few minutes. They refuse to budge. 'Nobody's listening to you,' says his mother. His brother starts falling off the sofa with laughter.

Will waits two nights for a moment when his family is out of the house so he can call Suzanne Widme. The moment never comes. The dance is only a few days away. He goes around the corner to the phone box. With trembling fingers, he dials Suzanne's number. Her father answers. He hangs up. He bangs his head against the glass for a few seconds, and then he rings back. This time Suzanne answers. He was prepared for her father, but not for her. He hangs up.

Will asks his best friend how to ask out Suzanne. 'Write her a note,' says his best friend. 'That way you don't have to be rejected in person.'

Well, that makes pretty good sense. Will would do anything to avoid public humiliation. He writes a note. It takes four hours, but in the end it is a masterpiece of coolness and economy: *Dear Suzanne, How about going to the dance with me? Yours truly, Will.* He carries it around with him all morning, checking every ten minutes or so to make sure that it's still in his pocket. Finally it's lunch time. He is about to walk over to her in the refectory and just slip it next to her cheese sandwich when a sobering thought occurs to him. What if she shows it to her friends? What if she passes it around the refectory? What if he misspelled her name or something and she thinks he's a complete dope? What if everyone starts laughing at him, not just Suzanne? He eats the note.

With two nights left before the dance, Will asks his father how to ask out a girl. 'Why don't you just pop round to her house and ask her in person?' says his father.

'Me?' asks Will, a little incredulous at the simple boldness of his father's method. 'Is that how you started dating Mum?'

'Something like that,' says his father.

Will puts on his jacket and marches over to Suzanne Widme's house. The lights are on so his hope that no one would be home is dashed. He stands in the bushes for thirty-six minutes, screwing up his courage. During this time he gets involved in listening to the television programme the Widme family is watching, so when it ends and he realizes that he's still in the bushes he has to start rehearsing his speech all over again. Finally, pretty sure that he's got the gist of it, he tip-toes to the front door. What if Suzanne doesn't answer the door? What if her sister, an Amazonian with the laugh of a goat, answers the door? Well, so what? he asks himself. There's no law against school friends of Suzanne's calling at her door. She's not going to know why he's there. He takes a deep breath and counts to ten. He takes another deep breath and counts to ten again. The door opens. It is Suzanne Widme's brother, on his way out to pump iron. 'Who the hell are you?' he wants to know. It may just be the way his arms are bulging through his T-shirt, but Suzanne's brother seems a little menacing. Will runs.

At school the next day, all the boys are talking about the girls they're taking to the dance the next evening. 'Hey, man,' they tell each other, 'she's crazy about me. I can tell. I bet she'll kiss me. I bet she'll beg me to ask her out again.' The other boys ask Will who he's taking to the dance. Will is casual. He dumps his chips on his lap and has to rush off to the boys' room to try and get the stain out of his trousers.

That night, in sheer desperation, Will calls Linda Peel. The minute he starts to dial the sitting-room goes quiet. Mrs Peel answers. Will asks for Linda. 'Will Williams,' he says, trying to keep his voice steady.

Will's brother starts to laugh. 'I'd change my name if I were you,' he sputters.

Linda Peel comes to the phone. 'Hi, Linda,' says Will.

'Who is this?' asks Linda.

'It's me, Will,' says Will.

'Will who?' asks Linda.

'Will Williams,' whispers Will.

His brother falls to the floor, clutching his sides.

'Will Williams?' Linda repeats. 'Do I know you?'

Does she know him? She's crazy about him. Maybe she's nervous, too. 'From English,' he says, having to speak a little loudly to be heard over his brother's giggles.

'You're in my English class?' Linda repeats. Not only isn't she very attractive, her hearing is lousy. 'Where do you sit?'

'Next to Mohammed,' says Will.

'Oh! *Will!*' exclaims Linda in recognition. 'What do you want? Didn't you get the homework?'

Now that he's talking to her, he realizes that he really likes Linda Peel. She's got those beautiful green eyes and she has a good sense of humour. 'No, no,' says Will, trying to cram as many words into a breath as he possibly can. 'I have the homework. I just wondered if you wanted to go to the dance with me tomorrow night.'

He is so convinced that Linda Peel would jump at the chance to go to the dance with him that it takes him a second before he realizes she has said no. 'Oh, gosh,' she says, 'I'm really sorry, Will, but I'm going away for the weekend with my parents right after school tomorrow.'

He knows she's lying. His stomach has started to digest itself, and tears are storming towards his eyes. Except for the continued hilarity of his brother, the silence in the sitting-room is exactly the same as the silence that will follow the end of the world. 'Oh, well, right, well, bye,' says Will and he hangs up the receiver. His mother is looking at him sympathetically. His father is memorizing the headlines on his newspaper. His brother is wetting himself. 'I didn't want to go with her anyway,' he screams, though no one asked. 'She's a dog.' He runs to his room. It will be several years before he ever asks out anyone else.

Two decades later, Will runs into Linda Peel on a TV set. He is a professional soundman now and she is Linda Ottoman, the great investigative reporter and drop-dead beauty. 'Will Williams!' she exclaims. She introduces him to the crowd of adoring admirers surrounding her. 'This is the boy who broke my heart,' she tells them. Everybody laughs. 'That sure is a turn-up for the books,' they agree. 'How did he manage that?' Linda explains how she'd waited all through secondary school for Will Williams to ask her out. 'And when he finally did,' she says with the devastating smile that has charmed psychopaths and prime ministers alike, 'I was so nervous I could barely speak.' Her admirers make surprised faces; who can imagine Linda Ottoman unable to speak? 'But that wasn't the worst part,' Linda continues. The worst part was that she had to turn him down because her family was going to visit her dying grandmother that weekend. 'I cried for weeks,' says Linda, who is laughing now. 'Every time the phone rang, I thought it might be Will, asking me out again, but he never did. He wouldn't even look at me in school anymore.'

Yesitis

Recent studies have proven that yesitis afflicts ninety per cent of the population at one time or another.

'Really? Ninety per cent? What is it exactly?'

Doctors are still baffled by yesitis, unsure of whether it is caused by environmental factors or is genetic in nature, but the symptoms are unmistakable: it makes you say yes when you want to say no.

Everyone in the office is going for a drink after work. You don't want to go. You're tired, you're not thirsty, you were looking forward to getting home and watching a documentary on aphids on television. 'Oh come on,' your workmates cajole you, 'just one drink.' It is never just one drink. You open your mouth to thank them for inviting you but you have to decline. But you don't want to hurt their feelings. You don't want them to think that you're unfriendly or too cheap to buy a round. You say, 'OK.'

The young man at the door wants you to buy cable TV. You don't want to. It's expensive. It's unnecessary. You hardly watch any television. What do you want with a pop video station? It's like watching hours of Levis commercials. 'Just let me come in and talk to you for a few minutes,' he says. You open your mouth to tell him that under no circumstances do you want him in your house, convincing you to buy something that you neither want nor need. But you don't want to appear ungracious. You don't want him to think you're unreasonable. You say, 'All right, you can come in, but not for long.'

Horace Flimmer, the salesman who leads the Christmas party in a spirited rendition of 'The Twist' each year, and whose idea of sophisticated wit is a cushion that farts when you sit on it, comes up to you at the coffee machine one day and says, 'Hey, doll, how about painting the town green, purple and blue with me Friday night?' He winks. You would rather be shopping on the high street on Christmas Eve than have to share a lift with Horace Flimmer. You would rather be stuck in a tube train with a woman who is worried that her sixteen cats will starve to death if she doesn't get home in the next five minutes than have to share a dinner table with Horace Flimmer. But, as unlikely as it is that Horace has any feelings that aren't connected to his stomach or his penis, you don't want to hurt them. 'What do you say, babe?' leers Horace. You say, 'Yes.'

Sex – The First Time

What separates man from the beasts?

No, not his seething intellect.

No, not his fear that his brother is going to receive a better birthday present from their parents than he did.

And though, yes, it is true that your average rhinoceros will not duck behind the sofa and pretend to be out when the Jehovah's Witnesses come to call, it isn't that either.

What separates man from the beasts is the fact that when it comes to sex, the beasts just do it, but man talks, worries, moans, fantasizes, and writes about it constantly, and then, instead of just doing it, he uses it to sell chocolates.

'Oh come on. It's not like no one ever has sex.'

Jean and John had been going together for several months. They liked each other. Although other people were driven insane by Jean's habit of looking elsewhere while they were talking to her, it never bothered John. Nor did his trait of answering every question with another question disturb Jean. Quite the contrary. They went to dinner together. They watched *Dallas* together. They visited stamp and kitchen exhibitions together. They went to the cinema and the theatre; to tennis matches and cricket games; to parks and museums. And eventually they decided to go to bed.

Jean, though thirty-three, still lived with her mother, who didn't really approve of sex in general, and certainly didn't approve of it for her daughter in particular. And John, though thirty-two, still shared a flat with three other people, two cats and a rabbit. Since his room was the one behind the kitchen, Jean and John decided that they would do the deed for the first time in a hotel.

Jean told her mother she was spending the night with her best friend, Binky. She told Binky that she was spending the night with John in The Old Oak Inn. (The Old Oak Inn was not only fifty miles away, but difficult to find even when you knew where it was, so the chances of Jean's mother stumbling upon them by chance seemed relatively remote.) She told Binky that she was feeling a little nervous. What would it be like? Would the earth move? Would the bed break? Would John, despite the affection and respect in which he held her, take one look at her thighs and bolt for the door? Binky told Jean to wear a sexy negligee, like they do in the movies, and to get into bed very quickly so John wouldn't have a chance to notice her thighs. Binky told Jean that the first time she slept with her boyfriend had been a magical, even spiritual experience, but that another friend of hers, Louise, has found the whole thing so painful and humiliating that she had become a Buddhist nun and was living in the Himalayas.

John told every man he knew that he was going to a hotel with Jean. 'We could just do it at my place,' he said in his I-am-a-man-of-the-world voice, 'but I wouldn't want to feel inhibited, you know . . .' (chuckling softly here to indicate 'because of her cries of passion, our mutual ecstasy, and/or vibrating love waves') '. . . on our first night just because somebody's boiling lentils in the kitchen.' Secretly, of course, and not to be admitted to anyone – especially not himself – what John was really afraid of was that one of his flatmates would hear Jean's sobs of disgust and/or disappointment. Or, even worse, her derisive laughter when she got a look at his erect member. In the few blue movies John had seen with the lads after several hundred pints of beer, erect members always looked like coppers' truncheons; it was difficult to reconcile that image with his own erect member, which looked a bit like a frankfurter, *sans* roll.

Anticipation grew as *the* weekend approached. John spent hours gazing at his penis and comparing it to the penises in the book he'd stolen from the library, *Making Love: The Ultimate Guide*. He worried about his receding hairline. He wondered if it was advisable to have a bottle of wine *before* they made love or if it would make him too tired. Was she going to be appalled by the hair on his back? Should he shave it off? But if he shaved it off and he and Jean eventually got married, he would have to secretly shave it off for the rest of his life. Jean spent hours slapping and pinching and bemoaning her thighs. Every evening she would lock herself in the bathroom and try on her negligee. She bought perfume. She practised inserting her diaphragm. 'Jean, love, what are you doing in there?' her mother would call at the bathroom door. 'It sounds like you're bouncing a ball around.'

But not all of this anticipation was laden with anxiety, of course. Being humans and not giraffes, John and Jean did, of course, have a pretty good idea of what sex was going to be like – assuming that the first glimpse of thighs and erect members didn't ruin everything. It was going to be . . . well, wonderful. Extraordinary. Life-changing. Astounding. There are people who never feel completely adult until they've hired their first cleaning lady, but John and Jean believed that it was the mutual orgasm that made the difference. They could hardly wait.

John and Jean became lost on their way to the hotel. Jean said, 'Take that little road off to the left. Yes, of course I'm sure, I'm looking at the map, aren't I?' and they wound up in the middle of a field of sheep. The car became quiet and they had to walk two miles to get petrol.

'I'm sorry,' whispered Jean when, smelling rather markedly of sheep dung, they eventually staggered up the steps of The Old Oak Inn. 'You're not mad at me, are you?'

'Shall we eat in our room?' asked John.

They decided not to eat in their room, because if they ate in their room the hotel owner, Mrs Melrose, would know that they weren't married. No aardvark in the history of the planet would ever think of this, but Jean had no trouble picturing Mrs Melrose bumping into her mother in Tesco's and, over the dairy cabinet, telling her about this unmarried couple who had come to her hotel for a dirty weekend and how she had had to throw them out. 'The girl's name wasn't Jean, was it?' her mother would shriek. 'Small and dark with rather thick thighs?'

Over dinner, John's confidence began to ebb a little. All the while he was talking to her about the carpet business, Jean was looking over his head at the couple behind them.

'Jean,' John kept saying, 'Jean, are you listening to me?'

'Of course I'm listening to you,' Jean answered. 'What makes you think I'm not listening to you?'

'Should we skip dessert?' asked John.

Jean went into the bathroom to change into her negligee. Although she had already taken a shower before dinner, to get rid of the smell of sheep dung, she decided to take a bath. Warm baths, she knew, were meant to get you in the mood. Perhaps it was the long walk to and from the petrol station, and having to push the car out of the sheep field because it got a little bogged down, but Jean fell asleep in the tub.

John, meanwhile, put on his pyjamas, took off his pyjamas, put on his pyjamas, wondered what Harrison Ford would do in a similar situation, and took them off again. He would wear just his Y-fronts and a smile. He glanced down. The smile vanished. It wasn't the family jewels behind those Y-fronts, it was the family sausage roll. He took off the Y-fronts and put on his pyjama bottoms. That was better. He'd read in *Penthouse* that women find just pyjama bottoms incredibly sexy. He smiled at himself in the mirror. Hair rose from his shoulders like waves from the ocean. Did he look incredibly sexy, or did he look like an ad for PG Tips? He put on a T-shirt. He'd read somewhere else that women found men in T-shirts incredibly sexy. He opened a bottle of wine he'd brought with them and poured himself a glass. He took off the T-shirt. He poured himself another glass. He took off the pyjama bottoms and got under the sheet. He looked at his watch. Had she gone out the bathroom window? He put his pyjama bottoms and the T-shirt back on and went to the door. 'Jean, love,' he called. 'Jean, are you all right in there?'

By the time Jean emerged from the bathroom, clean if a little wrinkled, and stinking of some perfume he'd never smelled on her before, John had opened the second bottle of wine.

He handed her a glass. He raised his own in a toast. 'To us!' he whispered, gazing seductively into her eyes. Or trying to gaze seductively into her eyes. Jean, in fact, was looking over his shoulder at the painting of a barn that hung on the wall.

'Darling,' said Jean, who unlike your average chinchilla had read a lot of romantic novels, 'you will be gentle with me, won't you?'

'You've got your thingamebob in, haven't you?' asked John.

John passed out for the forty-five minutes it took Jean to get her thingamebob in, but he rallied when she thumped into bed beside him and shook him by the shoulder.

Despite the fact that it didn't have that far to go, John had a little trouble getting it up. Then he had quite a bit of trouble getting it in. At last, sweating and gasping and bloody exhausted, he rolled from on top of Jean, feeling pretty pleased with himself after all. That wasn't so bad, for the first time.

'Darling,' Jean whispered, 'what's wrong? Aren't we going to do it?'

'Do you think you could move over, just a little, love?' asked John. 'You've got your elbow in my rib.'

The Penis Problem

Only a man could have conceived of the idea of penis envy. Let us be realistic, shall we? What's there to envy? Not a lot, most of the time. What you have is a rather unattractive, purplish appendage, that at its best looks like something prehistoric and aquatic and at its worst looks like it's been in an accident. This appendage is not only less than beautiful, it is sensitive, delicate and largely uncontrollable. The owners of penises (oddly enough, all men) spend more time worrying about them than anyone ever spent worrying about losing his hair or having fat thighs or whether or not some lunatic was going to drop an atomic bomb on Stoke Newington.

They worry that it's going to get caught in things, or that someone's going to want to cut it off. They worry that it's too small. They worry that someone's going to boff them in it. They worry that it's going to do something socially unacceptable in the middle of a tea party, film, or important meeting – something like poke up through their trousers like a tent pole or suddenly go off like Old Faithful. They worry that the other guys in the shower room are going to laugh at it. That girls are going to laugh at it. That it's going to catch something. That it'll go down too quickly. That . . .

She touches his shoulder. 'Don't worry about it, love,' she says. 'It happens to everyone.'

His back is to her. He stares at the pale yellow of the bedroom wall as another man might stare at the drab brick walls of his prison. 'Not to me it doesn't,' he says.

'Darling . . .' She pokes her head over his shoulder. She nibbles his ear.

She might as well be sticking pins under his eye lids. 'Get off, will you? Can't you see I'm upset?'

'But that's just the point,' she soothes. 'There's nothing to be upset about. All men are impotent from time to time.'

'I told you,' he hisses. 'I'm not impotent. I'm tired.'

She pats his shoulder. 'Of course you're tired,' she says.

He rolls over so quickly she bangs her head against the wall. 'And what's that supposed to mean?' he'd like to know. '*Of course you're tired*? You mean because we've been at it for so long? Is that what you mean?'

She straightens herself up, rubbing her head. 'Of course that's not what I mean. All I meant was that being tired is one of the causes of impotency.'

'How many times do I have to tell you?' The frustration of dealing logically with an illogical person makes him shout. 'I'm not impotent, I've had a hard day.' He looks her in the eyes. His mind, resting for the last hour or two, tries to function again. He frowns. 'Hey,' he says as the hormones ebb and the brainwaves slowly kick in, 'how do you know so much about it? Has this happened to *you* before?'

But she doesn't rise to the bait. 'I told you,' she says, 'I read about it in a magazine while I was waiting to have my hair done. And anyway,' she adds, 'everybody knows about it. It's a completely normal occurrence.'

'Then why hasn't it happened to me before, Mrs Knowitall, if it's so completely normal? Huh? Answer me that?'

'It just hasn't. Sometimes it does, and sometimes it doesn't.' She gives him a hug. 'Now why don't we get some sleep, and in the morning everything will be fine.'

She turns off the light. She wraps her arms around him.

He lays on his side in the dark, dead from the waist down. The alarm clock ticks away, slowly inevitably, just like his life. 'Umbghuhjud,' he says at last. And then a little louder, 'Umbghuhjud.'

'What?' she asks sleepily.

'Umbghuhjud.'

'I can't hear you, love. You're mumbling.'

'What if it happens again tomorrow?'

'It won't, darling. Now get some sleep.'

'But what if it does?'

'But it won't.'

'But what if it does?'

She props herself up on one elbow. 'Sweetheart, listen to me. Even if it does happen again tomorrow, it doesn't mean anything. It's just a temporary aberration. Maybe you're under some sort of strain.'

'Well that's bloody brilliant, isn't it?' he shouts. 'Of course I'm under some sort of strain. I can't get it up, can I? How much strain do you think I should have?'

'You're getting hysterical about nothing,' she says, her voice the only thing in the bed that is hard. 'Now stop whining and get some sleep.' She turns her back.

He lies on his side in the dark, imagining the future. There is none. What's the name for a situation like this? Ironic? Self-perpetuating? Catch-22? He can't get it up because he's under a strain. He's under a strain because he can't get it up. This sort of thing could go on for ever. 'Pumps,' he mutters into the heartless night. 'That's what they do. Pumps.'

She sits up, much the way he wishes his appendage would sit up. 'Now what are you going on about?' she asks.

'Pumps,' he repeats. 'They put a tube in your penis and they give you a little pump to make it stand up. Oh my God,' he wails, 'I'm not even forty and I've got the life of an inner tube. How can this be happening to me?'

'It's not happening to you,' she says. 'Nothing's happening to you.'

'Well, that's pretty obvious, isn't it?' he yells. 'I don't need you to tell me that.'

She holds his head between her hands and stares into his eyes. 'One time,' she says, slowly and carefully, enunciating beautifully. 'One time in thirty-three years. It's nothing to worry about.' She slides back under the covers. 'Now let's get some sleep.'

She's out like a light almost immediately. He lies there until dawn, testing.

Ego

An ego, like a gun, is not, in the abstract, a bad thing to have. In fact, it is a good thing. When it becomes a problem is when you have too much. Or, coincidentally, too little. How much do you have?

1. I am ____ wrong.
   a. almost never (The one time I was wrong was when I thought I'd made a mistake about something but I hadn't.)
   b. sometimes (As most people are.)
   c. almost always (I think.)

2. If I arrived late to the theatre I would ____ wait till the intermission before taking my seat.
   a. not (After all, it is *my* seat, isn't it?)
   b. of course (It's only polite.)
   c. Oh, I wouldn't go at all if I was late. Everybody would know.

3. I ____ make an entrance at parties.
   a. always (How could I not?)
   b. sometimes (But usually by accident.)
   c. would rather stand in the bushes all night than make an entrance at a party. (In fact, once I did stand in the bushes all night. I was hoping that a large crowd of people would arrive together and I'd be able to sneak in with them. Instead, I fell asleep.)

4. I have ___ met a person I couldn't charm.
   a. never (It's a gift, I know it. And I have it.)
   b. sometimes (In fact quite a few. Of course, I've also met a lot of people who haven't charmed me.)
   c. I don't think I've ever charmed anyone – well, no, I guess that isn't true. My dog likes me. Of course, everyone says he isn't very bright . . .

5. I am ___ attractive to members of the opposite sex.
   a. extremely (And that's an understatement caused by modesty. I mean, I *hate* to boast, but they follow me down the street.)
   b. averagely (You know, some people are attracted to me and some aren't.)
   c. not at all (I mean, someone was once attracted to me, but then they realized they'd made a mistake.)

6. People ___ notice me.
   a. always (How could they not?)
   b. don't always (It sort of depends.)
   c. never (Even my own mother once asked me who I was.)

7. I ___ get what I want.
   a. always (What else is life for?)
   b. sometimes
   c. I don't want anything.

8. ___ people who know me admire me.
   a. Most (The ones who don't are jealous.)
   b. Some
   c. What's to admire?

If your responses were largely b's, your ego is healthy but not too healthy. If you choose largely a's, your ego is probably the most noticeable thing about you. Did you select c a lot? Your ego needs a transfusion.

WHY ARE THEY SO STUPID/ UNREASONABLE/ ANNOYING . . . ?

Talking to Yourself

Every so often, you pass one on the street. Looking perfectly normal and respectable – not pushing a shopping trolley full of rubbish, not wearing newspapers wrapped around the feet, not smelling like the Hart and Hound on a Saturday night – someone walks by you talking to himself, nineteen to the dozen. Or herself, as the case may be. 'Oh, boy,' you say, shaking your head, 'I'm glad that's not me.'

Don't talk too soon.

The only reason most of us are under the illusion that we don't talk to ourselves, is because it's so natural to us that we don't know that we do it.

'I don't,' you boast. 'I never talk to myself.'

Never, as my paternal grandfather once had occasion to comment, is a long time to hang.

If you never talk to yourself, then when you're sitting at home, unable to move because the cat's asleep on your lap, listening to the radio, who is it that shouts back, 'You wouldn't know a good poet if he passed out on your lap!' when the presenter says something complimentary about Jim Morrison? Who is the person who comments on all the news stories and becomes enraged when two of the latest Phil Collins songs are played twice in an hour?

'Talking back to the radio isn't the same as talking to yourself.'

It is in most Western nations.

But all right, if you want to quibble, what about talking to the television? What about sitting by yourself, late at night, watching a sad and tender film of thwarted romance and broken hearts? As the train pulls away and the hero leans out of the window to take one last, longing look at the only woman he will ever love, and our heroine nobly blinks back the tears so he won't realize that she has sent him away not because she doesn't adore him, but because she does, someone in the sitting-room starts sobbing. 'Oh my God,' this person weeps, 'this is so lovely. It is just the saddest, most romantic story I've ever seen.' There is a rustle of tissues being pulled from a box and a chorus of sniffles. 'I just love the part where she sends him away the best,' this voice, muffled, continues. 'I really really do.' Now, if this voice doesn't belong to you, to whom does it belong?

'Talking to the television is exactly the same as talking to the radio. It doesn't count. I'm telling you I *never* talk to myself.'

You've never been about to walk into the road when the light started to change? You stepped back. The light didn't change. For some reason convinced that everyone else on the street has stopped to look at you and wonder to themselves, *What the hell is wrong with him? Why doesn't he cross, he has plenty of time?*, you started making faces and muttering to yourself, 'I suppose I should have crossed . . . well who knew it was going to take so long to change . . .' If you hadn't stepped back, but had decided to continue forward, the light would have changed instantly, the car that was waiting at the light would have roared into action, you would have jumped back so fast you landed on your bottom, and as you quickly got to your feet again you would have been heard to mumble to yourself, 'Oh, my, well he didn't waste any time, did he?'

'You didn't say anything about times of extreme stress and embarrassment. Everyone talks to themselves when they're embarrassed. You know, when you put your money in the coffee machine and nothing comes out. Or you trip on the pavement. Or you drop your handbag on the bus and your emergency tampon rolls down the aisle. I don't think you can count that either. Or times of exceptional stress. You know, when you're really mad at someone but you haven't told them so you fight with them while you're walking along by yourself.'

How about finding yourself standing in the middle of aisle three of the supermarket, staring up at the shelves and saying, 'Well, should I make the pasta, or should I make the stuffed vine leaves instead?' You mean you've never talked to yourself when buying a gift?

'Once or twice, but only at Christmas.'

And all the times you mutter hostilities at other drivers or wonder aloud where Finnerbopper Court is, was that Christmas too?

'Being in the car is like being in your own sitting-room, commenting on the nonsense the talk-show guests come up with. It doesn't count.'

And what about when you're trying to repair something difficult? Or you've been waiting for an hour for the bus or the train? Or they delay your flight for another three hours? Or the cash machine won't give you any money? Or the pay phone isn't working? Or you're in the bathroom?

Or, desperate circumstances (the washing machine broke three weeks ago and you haven't got around to having it repaired yet) have sent you into the launderette with four weeks' worth of dirty clothes. It's been a long time since you've been in the launderette and your natural terror of the place takes hold. You can't remember how to open the machine. You can't remember which compartment to put the detergent in. As you try to work this all out, someone starts talking to you. 'Is it the left compartment?' this someone asks. 'Yes, yes, I think it's the left. Ooops,' this someone says further, 'that was a little too much.' 'Hot wash, warm rinse?' asks this someone. 'Or warm wash, warm rinse?' This someone makes a tutting noise. 'What about cold wash, cold rinse? How much is this anyway?'

'It isn't I. I never talk to myself.'

Except if you're at home, in the car, embarrassed, or it's Christmas.

Nagging

Legend has it that my grandfather was nagged to death.

'Who told you that?' my grandmother interrupts. 'Mathilda? Did Mathilda tell you that?'

Well, not to death exactly, but to disappearance. One day he went out for a hinge for the door he was fixing and he never came back.

'It was Mathilda, wasn't it?' says my grandmother. 'I can tell.'

My grandmother herself, on the other hand, had always maintained that there is no such thing as a nagger, there are just people who won't do what they were told.

'Grandma,' I remember saying, 'there is a difference between a person who asks you to do something and a nagger.'

'What?' asked my grandmother. 'Are you going to tell me? What's the difference?'

'Wait a minute, grandma,' I mumbled, 'just let me finish this piece of toffee.'

'What?' my grandmother repeated, her voice snapping with impatience. 'I thought you were going to tell me what the difference was.'

'About an hour and a half,' I choked.

I was, of course, being kind. Though naggers do differ from non-naggers in that they expect whatever they've asked you or asked you to do to be answered or done before they've asked it, there are other points of distinction.

Would You Remind My Grandfather of Someone He Once Wed?

Select the answer that is most applicable to you.

1. Your spouse/child/flatmate comes down to breakfast. The first thing you say is:
   a. 'Good morning.'
   b. 'I hope you turned off the light in the bathroom.'

2. The second thing you say is:
   a. 'Had a good sleep?'
   b. 'Don't forget, you promised to take out the rubbish this morning.'

3. The third thing you say is:
   a. 'Would you like some juice?'
   b. 'Try not to leave the top off the toothpaste today, all right?'

4. Your spouse/child/flatmate finishes her/his cereal. As the spoon clinks against the bowl, you say:
   a. 'How about some toast?'
   b. 'Don't think you're going to leave that bowl sitting there for me to clear away.'

5. Your secretary, a very busy person, has promised to get you a refill of staples for your stapler. Until she fills out the appropriate requisition, has it approved by the keeper of the supplies, and travels the twelve floors to the basement to get it, she has lent you her stapler, just in case you discover something on your desk that urgently requires a staple. You
   a. thank her politely, and the next day, when she has a chance to get your refill and even put it in your machine for you, you thank her again.
   b. say, 'You haven't forgotten about those staples, have you?' every time you pass her desk or she passes yours.

6. There is a programme on television tonight that you really want to watch. You'd like to watch it with someone; with the person who shares your home, actually. You say, 'How about watching the documentary on East European car dealers with me tonight? It's meant to be terrific.' Your home-sharer says, 'I'd rather catch up on my correspondence.' You

a. watch the programme by yourself, though you do occasionally shout out into the other room, 'This is really terrific, love. You're going to be sorry you missed it.'

b. say, 'Are you sure?' Your home-sharer says, 'Yes, I'm sure.' 'You really should see this,' you say. 'I should think someone in your line of work would find it especially fascinating.' Your home-sharer says, 'I really don't feel like watching television tonight.' 'You can write letters any night,' you say, 'why don't you watch the programme with me.' 'Because I really don't feel like it,' your home-sharer replies. 'It'll be fun,' you coax. 'I know you'll enjoy it.' 'Look,' says your home-sharer, 'read my lips. I do not want to watch a documentary on East European car dealers.' 'Not even for me?' you ask. 'Not even for you,' is the answer. 'Just watch for ten minutes,' you plead. 'Then if you don't like it you can go write your letters.' A faint note of desperation, to which you are oblivious, creeps into your home-sharer's voice. 'I don't want to watch even three minutes of this idiotic programme,' says the voice. 'Ten minutes,' you argue, 'what's ten minutes?'

If any of your answers were b, you are a hopeless nag, and should be careful of asking anyone close to you to fix the door in the hallway more than seventeen times in one morning.

Babies

No one can really perfect their neurotic tendencies without the benefit of children. Especially small children. What could better sharpen your abilities at self-delusion, abstract terror, theoretical fear, and eccentric behaviour than a creature who either can't communicate its feelings, hopes and aspirations to you, or isn't interested when you try to communicate yours to him?

The Baby Cries

The baby cries. You have just fed the baby, changed the baby, bundled him up in his cute little pyjamas, bounced him around in your arms for a few minutes and pointed out the brightly coloured clowns on the wallpaper of his room, and put him down for his nap. You know he's tired, because he's been rubbing his little eyes and yawning for the last fifteen minutes. He practically passed out in his stewed prunes. You tip-toe out of the room as his eyelids droop. You take one step towards the sitting-room. The baby cries.

Five of the baby books you read during your pregnancy told you that you should let the baby cry. Crying is good for him. You don't want to spoil him, do you?

You let him cry. And cry he does. Even if you stand in the hall cupboard, muffled by the winter coats, you can hear him crying.

Why is he crying?

Six of the baby books you read during your pregnancy told you that you shouldn't let the baby cry. Crying isn't good for him. You don't want him to think you don't love him, do you?

You go back in. You tell him you love him. He doesn't care. You check his clothes. Nothing pinching or biting. He cranks up the volume. Maybe he's too hot. 'Are you too hot?' you ask him.

In answer, he starts turning purple. Maybe he's too cold. You feel his tiny hands, jammed into angry fists. 'Are you too cold?' you ask him. He starts to scream.

Maybe he's still hungry. 'I know,' you say, 'you're still hungry.' You hustle him into the kitchen. The kitchen doesn't seem to make him any happier than the bedroom. If it is possible for a child who has not yet seen so much as a dog to do a stunningly accurate impersonation of a wolf howling, then your child is doing so. You show him his bottle. He scorns his bottle. You show him his favourite rusk. He scorns that too. 'What is it sweetheart?' you coo. 'Are you bored? Would you like to go for a walk?'

With a great deal of effort, you manage to get his wriggling, kicking, furious little body into its jacket and cap. You drop him in his buggy. You head for the great outdoors.

He doesn't want to go for a walk. His crying is so loud that you can't hear the traffic. His crying is so loud that everyone on the street – even the three guys dressed like SS troopers with skulls tattooed on their necks – turns to look at you, suspiciously. You can see the questions in their eyes. Does she beat that baby? Does he have a pin sticking in him? Has she been denying him mashed bananas and milk? Is he ill? Your own face turns crimson with shame and doubt. Has he got hold of a pin somehow and stuck it into himself because you're such a bad mother? Have you been inadvertently holding back on the bananas and milk? Is he ill?

My God! you think. That's it! He's ill. You spin around and run back home. The baby cries the entire way. You scoop him up in your loving arms and race to the phone. You know the doctor's number by heart. 'Hello?' you say when the receptionist answers. 'This is The Baby's Mother.'

'I know,' says the receptionist. 'I recognized the voice.' You're not sure, because the baby's making so much noise, but it almost sounds as though the receptionist is not supressing several heavy sighs. 'So what is it this time?' the receptionist wants to know. 'Does he look pale? Does he look too swarthy? Did he sleep an hour too long? Did he miss his nap? Does it look like he's cross-eyed? Are his ears different sizes? Did he say "Constantinople" again? Are you still worried that he feels hostility towards his teddy bear? Is he still refusing to wear red?'

'He's crying,' you say.

'Crying?' repeats the receptionist.

'Yes,' you say. 'Crying.'

'It is one of the things that babies do do, you know,' the receptionist points out.

But you're ahead of her. 'For no reason?' you ask with just an edge of sarcasm.

'Oh, I'm sure there's a reason,' says the receptionist helpfully. 'You probably drive him as crazy as you drive me.'

The Baby Has to Be Left with a Babysitter

For the first several months of the baby's life you managed not to have to leave him for even an hour with some stranger who couldn't possibly love, understand, or care for him as well as you do. In other words, a babysitter. You have turned down invitations to parties, dinners and celebrity galas with one feeble excuse after another, all because you didn't want anyone to think you were child-fixated or over-protective, not, of course, that you are. You aren't. You're just cautious and responsible.

But now you have been asked to attend an awards dinner in your honour. Children are not invited, not even ones who own a formal T-shirt with a black tie printed on it.

'He is almost a year,' says your husband. 'That should be old enough to leave him with someone.'

'And it's only for a couple of hours,' you add.

'That's right,' says your husband. 'What could happen in a couple of hours.'

You and your husband look at each other. He could choke, say your husband's eyes. He could drown, say yours. He could suffocate, your husband's eyes continue. He could get his head caught between the bars of his crib, say yours. What if he doesn't stop crying? suggest your husband's eyes. What if the babysitter starts talking on the phone and doesn't hear him crying? your eyes counter. What if he throws himself out of bed? your husband's eyes would like to know. What if he stops breathing? scream yours. What if he's kidnapped? What if the house catches on fire? What if he gets hold of something poisonous and drinks the whole bottle? What if he sticks his little finger in an outlet? What if he pulls a lamp down on his head? What if he wants tapioca and there's no tapioca in the pantry? What then?

Your husband comes up with a plan. It is not foolproof, of course, but it's not bad. The babysitter will have to pass a first-aid course before she's allowed to look after your baby. Including life saving. She will have to show a certificate before she can stay with your child.

Your mother isn't too happy about this. 'I raised six children of my own without passing any first-aid course,' your mother grumbles. 'And nothing happened to them.'

'You were lucky,' say you and your husband.

The night of the dinner arrives. The babysitter arrives, with her Red Cross certificate in hand. You let her in. You explain to her about nappies and bottles and night lights and all that sort of thing, and she says, 'Susan, if you tell me one more time how to change a baby I'm going to punch you on the nose.'

Eventually, after everything has been checked and rechecked

several times, you leave. You go out to the car and you drive about a block. You pull over to the first phone-box you come to and phone home. 'We just wanted to make sure that everything's OK,' you say.

'Everything's fine,' says your mother.

You telephone from the restaurant lobby. 'How's it going?' you ask.

'No change in the last fifteen minutes,' says your mother.

You and your husband take your seats at the head table. You say hello to several people, take two sips of wine, and excuse yourself to go to the ladies. You ring your mother. 'Everything all right?' you say. 'You know where his bottle's kept, don't you?'

'He's sleeping,' says your mother.

You hurry back to the table. 'He's sleeping!' you whisper to your husband.

'Sleeping?' echoes your husband. He glances at his watch. 'He can't be sleeping already,' says your husband. 'He never goes to sleep before eleven.'

'He's probably just pretending,' you tell him. 'I'll call back in an hour and make sure.'

You call back in ten minutes. He's still asleep. 'Are you sure he's breathing?' you ask your mother. 'He never goes to sleep this early. What did you do to him?'

'I put him in bed,' says your mother. She sounds a little tetchy.

'She says he's still sleeping,' you whisper to your husband when you regain the table.

'Is she sure he's breathing?' asks your husband. 'Did she hold a mirror up to his mouth?'

'I'll ring back as soon as we've had our starters,' you assure him.

You ring back before the starters have been served. The line's engaged. You try again. The line's engaged. You go back to the table. As soon as you finish your first course, you telephone home again. The line's still engaged. You call the operator. The line's not engaged, it's off the hook.

'Off the hook?' gasps your husband. 'Do you think someone tried to steal the baby? Do you think in the struggle the phone was knocked off the hook?'

You're pulled over for speeding on the way home. You explain to the officer that you left your baby with an incompetent stranger who has either wilfully taken the phone off the hook or has been set upon by kidnappers and that that is why you were tearing up the high street like a reindeer out of hell. He gives you a police escort. You, your husband, and officers Burke and Brown, run up the stairs to your flat. There's no time to waste with keys. They break down the door. The sitting-room is empty!

You start to weep. 'My God!' you sob, 'they've taken my baby.'

At the sound of your voice, your mother appears from the kitchen with a beer and a sandwich in her hand. She seems surprised to see you. And pretty astounded to see the cops. 'Susan!' she shouts. 'What's happened?'

'It's the baby!' you choke. 'He's been kidnapped!'

'Kidnapped?' says your mother. 'What are you talking about "kidnapped"?'

'Who is this woman?' asks Officer Brown.

'What does the baby look like?' asks Officer Burke from the bedroom.

'He's beautiful,' you sob. 'He's the most beautiful baby in the world.'

'One of his ears is bigger than the other,' says your mother.

'Is this him?' asks Officer Burke, reappearing with the baby in his arms.

'That's him!' you and your husband cry as one. 'Thank God he's safe!'

'It's all right, darling,' you tell the baby as you lift him from Officer Burke's arms. 'Mummy's here.'

The baby starts to cry.

Dealing with the Public

Cinema Goer: I'd like four adult tickets, please.
Ticket Person: For which theatre?
Cinema Goer: Four, please.
Ticket Person: For which theatre?
Cinema Goer: What?
Ticket Person: Which film is it that you'd like to see?
Cinema Goer: (turning away from ticket person and shouting to someone behind her) What film is it we're seeing, Doug?

Gina:	Theatre 1.
Bob:	No, it's not 1, it's 2.
Doug:	Did you want popcorn, love, or just a drink?
Ticket Person:	So which is it, 1 or 2?
Cinema Goer:	(beginning to scream) Doug, for heaven's sake! Which film are we seeing?
Gina:	You're right, Bob, it's 2.
Bob:	(shaking his head) No, no, Gina. You're right. It's 1.
Doug:	(screaming a little himself) Popcorn, or what?
Ticket Person:	Madam, if you don't mind, you're holding up the queue. Just tell me what you think the film you want to see is about.
Cinema Goer:	Spacemen. (she turns to her friends) It's about aliens, isn't it?
Bob:	No, we decided not to see the aliens one, remember? We finally agreed on the thriller.
Gina:	I never agreed on the thriller. I hate thrillers. All that gratuitous violence. I thought I made it clear that if you want to see the thriller I'll go by myself to the romantic comedy about the prostitute who turns out to be a ghost.
Ticket Person:	We're not showing that film tonight.
Cinema Goer:	You're not showing that film? But that's the film we wanted to see.
Doug:	(coming up with four popcorns and four drinks) Sweetheart, that's not the film you wanted to see. You wanted to see the one about the aliens. Only Bob already saw it.
Bob:	That's what I've been trying to tell her, Doug. We agreed to see the thriller.
Gina:	(to ticket person) Just give me one for the ghost.
Ticket Person:	Madam, as I've already said, we're not showing –
Cinema Goer:	But I hate thrillers, Doug. You know that. (to ticket person) Make that two for the ghost.
Ticket Person:	(rather loudly) The ghost film was last week!
Doug:	(chuckling) I see what the problem is, chaps.
Bob:	What?
Gina:	What?
Cinema Goer:	What?

Ticket Person: What?
Doug: We're at the wrong cinema! (everybody laughs, except ticket person and the thirty-eight people behind them in the queue).

Directions

I was walking down the street with my mother one evening when a stranger stopped us to ask for directions. 'Excuse me,' said the stranger, 'but I was wondering if you could tell me how to get to Ridermill Street.'

My mother had lived in the village for forty years. I had lived in the village for nineteen. It was not a large village.

'Of course,' said my mother.

'No problem,' said I.

'Go down to the end of this street and turn left,' said my mother. 'Then just go straight until you come to the hedge that's cut like a spade –'

'Mum,' I interrupted. 'It's not a spade, it's a shamrock. And anyway, he'd be a lot better off going right on Hillock and then making that sharp left past the second petrol station.'

'It's the third petrol station,' said my mother. 'You always forget about Mason's.'

'But Mason's is closed in the summer,' I objected. 'And it isn't really a petrol station, it just has the one pump.'

'It sells petrol,' said my mother. She turned back to the stranger. 'Make a right at the spade,' my mother continued. 'Not the first right but the one just next to it, and go along there for a mile or so.'

'Mum,' I said, 'he wants the first right, not the second. If he takes the second he'll hit that fork by Wynot's. People always get confused at that fork.'

'He won't get confused if he remembers that he wants to go as though he's taking the road to Huntleigh but then he has to turn off right away on to that dirt road.' She smiled at the stranger. 'You don't mind bullocks, do you?' she asked sweetly.

'Mind them?' asked the stranger.

'Once you pass the bullocks you'll see a tiny lake on your left,' said my mother.

'Mum,' I sighed, 'you're going to get him lost. You give the worst directions of anyone I know. Remember that time you gave Dad directions to London and he wound up in Brighton?'

'That wasn't my fault,' said my mother. 'It's because he never pays attention. He nods away while you're giving him the directions and then he goes off the opposite way. And besides, London's not really all that far from Brighton. It's an easy mistake to make.'

'I'm sorry I mentioned it,' I said. 'The point is, that there's a lake on the right as well.'

'But it's not the lake on the right that concerns us,' my mother pointed out. 'It's the one on the left. Once he sees that he knows he has to keep a sharp eye out for Trellis Cottage.'

'Holly,' I corrected her.

'Holly?' said my mother and the stranger as one.

'Yes,' I explained. 'Ridermill runs directly behind Holly Cottage.'

'Ridermill?' said my mother. She turned to the stranger, scowling slightly. 'I thought you said you wanted Ridgehill,' she said.

In the end, we managed to give the stranger directions to Ridermill.

'Got it?' asked my mother briskly.

The stranger nodded.

'No more questions?' asked my mother.

The stranger shook his head.

He put the car in gear. He took off the brake. He roared off in the wrong direction.

Eating Out

The scene is a small but obviously popular restaurant. It is dimly lit and the decor is tasteful. A wonderful aroma – or several wonderful aromas – fills the room. The front door opens and a couple enters. Their names are Arnie and Jane. They are on a blind date.

Arnie: I think you're going to really like this place, Janet. The food's terrific.

Jane: Jane. (and then, optimistically) Oh, I'm sure I am.

Arnie: (to the waiter as he leads them to a table in the middle of the room) Not too close to the door, if you don't mind.

Waiter: (pulling out the table he'd been heading towards all the time, which, in fact, is the only table for two available) Of course not, sir.

Arnie: Don't you have anything in the corner? (turning to Jane) Wouldn't you prefer something in the corner, Janet?

Jane: Jane. Oh no, really, this is fine.

Arnie: Inside or outside?

Jane: Well, I . . . um . . . well, inside I suppose.

Arnie: (lowering his voice and touching her arm) Um, Janet, would you mind terribly if I sat on the inside? I have this thing about having my back against the wall . . . I mean, it's nothing, really, but if you wouldn't mind too much . . .

Jane: Jane. Oh, no, of course, sure, I just thought . . .

Arnie: (shuffling into the seat against the wall) You're sure this is all right, now, aren't you Janet? I wouldn't want to put you out or anything.

Jane: (giving up) Oh, no really. It's fine.

Arnie: (the waiter has given them menus and vanished into the air) So, Janet, what would you like? Have anything you want, I have American Express.

Jane: Well, what would you recommend?

Arnie: (laughs) Everything. No, seriously, the salmon is excellent. And the pasta with artichokes is out of this world.

Jane: But does it have cream? I'm worried about my cholesterol level, so I'm not eating cream.

Arnie: In that case, the risotto or the linguini with lightly sautéd vegetables might be just the ticket. (he looks up at the waiter who has come to take their orders) I don't think we're quite ready yet.

Jane: (not having noticed that the waiter has come and gone) I had rice yesterday, though. How big are the portions here? I'm trying to watch my weight, so if the portions are very large . . .

Arnie: The portions are generous, Janet, but don't forget, you can always take home whatever you don't eat. If you have them put the dressing on the side rather than on the salad, you can even take any leftovers of that home, too.

Jane: What's the chicken like? I guess it has a lot of butter, right?

Arnie: The grilled jumbo shrimp is quite nice.

Jane: (shaking her head at the waiter) No, I'm not ready yet.

Arnie: How about a drink while we decide? Janet, would you like a drink?

Jane: A drink?

Arnie: Wine?

Jane: Oh, that would be nice.

Arnie: Red or white?

Jane: Oh, um. Well . . . white's less fattening.

Arnie: (to the waiter) A bottle of the house red.

Jane: (still peering at the menu) What's the pasta primavera like?

Arnie: It has cream.

Jane: It doesn't say it has cream. It says it's an aromatic blend of fresh vegetables and herbs in a delicate wine sauce.

The waiter comes with the wine and a basket of bread. Arnie sends back the wine because it's too cool. The waiter brings another bottle of wine, of the same temperature.

Arnie: Excellent.

Waiter: Are we ready to order now?

Jane: (wiping the rim of her wine glass with her napkin) I just want to know, does the pasta primavera have cream in it?

Waiter: The pasta primavera is an aromatic blend of fresh vegetables and herbs in a delicate wine sauce.

Jane: I'll have the grilled shrimp. And a mixed salad, with the dressing on the side. Are there any onions in the salad?

Waiter: Spring onions.

Jane: No onions in the salad. And green olives rather than black.

Arnie: I'll have the pasta with artichokes and the mixed salad, with the dressing on the side.

Waiter: And to start?

Arnie: Janet?

Jane: Ooh. (She frowns at the menu) I'll have the beans and tuna. But then instead of the shrimp I'll have the risotto. It doesn't have onions in it, does it?

Waiter: Very small onions.

Jane: (smiling ruefully) I just can't stand the texture of onions.

Waiter: They're chopped very small.

Jane: I'll have the ensalada tricolore to start and the grilled shrimp.

Waiter: And the *Signor*?

43

Arnie: I'll have the antipasto to start.

Jane: Oh, I didn't see that. (turning to waiter) Does that have –

Waiter: (quickly) I'll tell them to leave out the onions.

Jane: Fish with heads in it?

Waiter: Excuse me?

Jane: (making a face at Arnie) I can't stand those little eyes looking up at me.

Waiter: No, *Signorina*. No heads.

Jane: But it does have fish?

Waiter: (pointing to menu) Yes.

Jane: I'll have the antipasto and the chicken cacciatore.

Waiter: You're sure?

Jane: No, you're right. I'll have the ensalada tricolore and the grilled shrimp.

Waiter: Excellent. One antipasto, one ensalada tricolore; one pasta with artichokes and one grilled shrimp.

Arnie: And two salads, with dressing on the side.

Jane: And no onions in my salad and only green olives.

Waiter: Two salads, dressing on the side, no onions, no green olives. Anything else?

Jane: I'll have the antipasto, too, and the chicken cacciatore. But I don't want hard-boiled eggs with my antipasto.

The waiter whips the menus out of their hands and vanishes once more. In time, he returns with their starters. Arnie sends back the antipasto because the eggs are dry.

Arnie: (winking) I guess you were wise not to have the eggs, Janet.

Jane: (picking through the antipasto for any sign of an onion) It's the cholesterol. I have to be very careful.

When the waiter brings their main course, Arnie sends his pasta back because it's overcooked.

Jane: (taking a bite of her chicken) Butter.

Arnie: Butter?

Jane: (nodding) I definitely taste butter.

Arnie: (having summoned the waiter) There's butter in the chicken cacciatore.

Waiter: (shaking his head) No, no butter. The chicken she is sautéd in the finest olive oil.

Jane: I taste butter. (looks to Arnie) My body is so sensitive to it. It's like radar.

Chef: (summoned by waiter) I promise you, *Signorina*, there is no butter in the chicken cacciatore.

Jane: (frowning thoughtfully and making little smacking sounds as she tastes the chicken again) No? (she clutches her throat, as understanding attacks her) Oh, my God! I know what it is! It's onions. Are there onions in the tomato sauce?

Chef: (looking as though he wishes he'd become a doctor, after all) Of course there are onions in the tomato sauce. Have you ever heard of anyone making tomato sauce *without* onions?

Jane: My mother.

Arnie: (sampling the pasta the waiter has just brought him, which is, in fact, his original plate that's been sitting under the hot lamp for the last five minutes) Ah, that's better.

Waiter: (some time later) And for dessert?

Arnie: Janet?

Jane: Oh, the raspberry Napoleon.

Waiter: (raising one eyebrow) The *Signorina* does realize that the Napoleon is made with cream and puff pastry, doesn't she?

Jane: It's in savoury things that I can't have cholesterol. (to Arnie) I just love raspberry Napoleons.

Arnie: I'll have the chocolate gateau.

Jane eats two raspberry Napoleons. Arnie sends the chocolate gateau back.

Entertaining

Very few people who don't have maids, cooks and a fleet of back-up servants actually enjoy entertaining, and even most of them don't like it either.

Why?

Because entertaining is the social function from hell.

How so?

Let's take it step by step.

Step 1. You decide to entertain. You look up one evening when there is nothing much happening and you think, I know, I'll have a dinner party. I'll invite all the people who have had me over in the past few months and whom I haven't invited back. I'll get rid of a half dozen obligations at once.

Step 2. You ring up the six people you've decided to invite and you invite them. For a week on Friday. Sara can't make it on Friday, nor can Lance. Sara can make the Saturday or the Thursday. Lance can make the Saturday. So you change it to the Saturday. You ring the other people back. Nadine can't make Saturday. Nor can Bobby. They can both make Thursday. Lance will have to go. You ring everyone back and make it for Thursday. You replace Lance with Vinnie. It is only as you are making sure that Vinnie isn't one of those difficult vegetarians who don't eat fish or chicken that you realize that you can't make Thursday.

Step 3. You finally arrange a night on which everyone can come. It's six weeks in the future, but it is a date. You can now start worrying about what you'll serve. Something simple. Maybe that nice pasta dish you had at Nadine's that she said was so simple. And a salad. And garlic bread. What about a starter? Avocado and prawns. It's dead easy and it's delicious, too. You can't have avocado and prawns, Vinnie is one of those difficult vegetarians who doesn't eat fish. Not even very small fish. You'll start with soup. Soup and then lasagne. Lasagne's better than pasta because you can make it ahead and have so much more time to spend with your guests. You write out a list and tape it to the refrigerator.

Step 4. By the time the weeks have passed and you are ready to do the shopping for this dinner, you have changed the menu no less than sixteen times. You are back to lasagne. But when you get to the supermarket, they are out of lasagne. How can they be out of lasagne? You go up and down every aisle – twice – just to make sure that you haven't missed the lasagne. You haven't, they don't have any. What can you use instead of lasagne noodles? Macaroni? Egg noodles? You've got it! You'll get those round tubes and cut them in half. But what if they're too small? Everyone will wonder why the lasagne noodles are so short. You'll make Nadine's simple and delicious pasta.

Step 5. You clean the house the night before. On the day of the party, you tell your boss you have a dental appointment so you can get ready. You rush home and start to cook. You forgot to buy beans, but it is too late to do anything about that now, you only have four hours before your guests arrive. You substitute peas. You didn't buy enough tomatoes. You throw in a little tomato juice. You can't find the lettuce. Where could it be? Lettuce doesn't have a life of its own, it

46

pretty much stays where you put it. You check the refrigerator again. Where did you put it? You open the freezer. There's the lettuce. If you'd known this was going to happen you could have got beans. Maybe you should get a tin of beans. You race down to the corner and buy a tin of beans and a head of lettuce. You break two bowls while you are trying to make the salad dressing, set the table, and run a bath. You nearly take off the tip of your finger trying to slice the cucumber. You wrap a paper towel around your finger and plough on. You look at the clock. Good grief! They'll be here in an hour and you're still in your office clothes and there are things in your hair. You jump into the bath. You jump out again when you realize that you can smell the sauce gently scorching. You turn off the sauce and go back to the bath. You hurriedly dry and dress yourself. You stand at the head of the table, counting forks and plates and napkins and wondering what you've forgotten. Knives. Spoons. Salt and Pepper. At last everything is ready. All you have to do is put the bread in the oven, heat up the sauce and cook the pasta. You pour yourself a glass of wine. And that's when you notice the wine glasses. They look like snails have been walking over them. With not a second to lose, you wash them all. You collapse on to the sofa with your glass of wine. You drink it. You drink another. You check your watch. Why has no one arrived? Wasn't Nadine giving Sara and Vinnie a lift? Maybe she ran out of petrol. Nadine's always running out of petrol. It's because she's convinced that the gauge is wrong. What about the other three? Bobby's always late for everything. The reason he's still single is because he missed his own wedding. And Max? Max is a workaholic. He's probably still at the office, muttering to himself, 'I'll just finish this, and then I'll go.' Cindy? Cindy's probably still getting dressed. You know what Cindy's like. It's OK, you're panicking over nothing. You'll give them another half hour. You have some more wine and a couple of peanuts. Maybe something's happened. An accident. An accident involving all six of them? No, not Max, he's still at the office, working. And not Cindy, she's still getting dressed. And Bobby's probably just leaving the house. You turn on the radio to see if there's been an accident nearby. You can't find the news station. All you can find is a phone-in. People seem to be pretty upset about the relationship between the Care Bears and Satan. You assume you've had too much wine and are misunderstanding. You telephone Nadine. 'Hi,' says Nadine. 'What's up?'

'What's up?' you gasp. 'What do you mean what's up? Why aren't you here?'

'Here where?' asks Nadine.

'Here at my dinner party,' say you.

'Is it tonight?' asks Nadine. 'I thought it was next week.'

Guests

There's an old Norwegian saying that goes: Guests bring with them more than fifteen suitcases, their children, their dirty laundry, a jar of pickled pigs' feet and the dog.

When I was a child, I didn't understand this saying. 'What more *could* they bring and still fit it all in the car?' I'd ask my grandmother.

My grandmother would smile. 'Just wait and see,' she'd say. 'When you're older you'll understand.'

Guests bring with them all the quirks and eccentricities that you don't notice when you only see someone twice a year for dinner. Of course, you notice some of their quirks and eccentricities when you encounter them twice a year over an Italian dinner. You notice that they put soy sauce on their lasagne. You notice that she can't sit at the table for longer than two seconds without remembering something else she forgot in the kitchen. You notice that he's cheap with the wine and that the children interrupt every conversation. You notice that there isn't one piece of furniture that hasn't been ripped to shreds by the cat and that they don't seem to mind that this same cat has a habit of walking across the table in the middle of a meal.

'Lordy, Lordy,' you say. 'How many more quirks and eccentricities could there be? What haven't you noticed?'

The Things You Don't Notice Until Someone Becomes a Guest in Your Home

1. How many times a day they bathe.
2. What they do with their wet towels.
3. How much soap/shampoo/talcum powder/bath oil it takes to get them looking like that.

4. How early they go to bed.
5. How late their children go to bed.
6. How many pillows they use.
7. How fond they are of fresh air.
8. The number of times they get up in the night to go to the bathroom.
9. That they sleepwalk.
10. Where they go when they sleepwalk.
11. That they can consume half a loaf of bread and a pound of cheese and roast beef while asleep.
12. That they have a recurring nightmare which takes place during World War III while a nuclear bomb is being dropped on Newcastle that makes them scream quite loudly.
13. How much they talk in their sleep.
14. What they say.
15. How much they and their children eat in one sitting.
16. What they eat.
17. That neither of them ever lets the other complete a whole sentence.
18. How early their children get up.
19. That she's allergic to cotton.
20. That you don't own anything that they don't have the better model of.
21. That she's in touch with an Egyptian slave who lived 2,000 years before Christ.
22. That this slave had a pretty good sense of humour.
23. That some people do make love every night.
24. Who they blame for World War II.
25. What they feed their dog, and when and how.
26. Where their dog sleeps.
27. That their dog doesn't have his own bowl.
28. Why they named their dog Spot.
29. The way in which they think a cat should be held.
30. How important the telephone is in their lives.
31. How upset they get when you pour the milk in after the tea.
32. How much their children dislike being touched.
33. What not being overly modest about your body really means.
34. How much it is possible for one man to complain.
35. How much it is possible for that man's children to complain.

36. How long it can take someone to peel a potato.
37. That they think the room meant in the phrase 'room temperature' is the kitchen.
38. That you never really appreciated what frugal meant before.
39. That true greed is asking for your second slice of pizza when you haven't even started to eat your first.
40. That some people really believe that they're never wrong.

Advice

When it comes to advice, the world breaks down into two major groups: those who seek advice that they have no intention of following and those who give advice that no one has sought.

'Excuse me?' you say.

It's true. I know it doesn't make any sense, but what does?

Let's say, for instance, that Andrea wants to go to Thailand for her holiday. She knows she can't really afford it. She knows she should stay home and take care of her boyfriend, Charlie, who's been in a plaster cast for the last month, but she really wants to go to Thailand and she can get a special deal because it's October and no one else wants to go to Thailand in October. But how can she justify the expense and the bad mood it's going to put Charlie in?

'By talking it through with Charlie and her bank manager in a mature and reasonable fashion?'

No way. She asks for advice.

Andrea asks everyone she knows for their opinion.

'Do you think I should go to Thailand in October?' she asks her friends.

'Do you think I should go to Thailand in October?' she asks her sisters and brothers.

'Mum,' she says, 'do you think that when October comes I should go to Thailand?'

'Dad,' she says, 'don't you think I have a right to happiness?'

Andrea's friends say, 'To tell you the truth, Andrea, it doesn't seem like a very good idea. Thailand's rainy in October, and even though you've got a bargain on accommodation it's going to be an expensive trip.'

Her sisters and brothers say, 'It'd probably be better if you waited,

Andrea. Then you could go with Charlie and at a time of year when the hotel's not under four feet of water.'

Her father says, 'No, I do not think you should go, not even if they pay you. Absolutely not.'

Her mother thinks she has a right to happiness, but not in a bamboo hut with primitive toilet facilities.

And then, just when she's looking around for another set of family and friends, Andrea happens to bump into someone she used to know from school on the bus.

'So what have you been up to?' asks Andrea after this person remembers her as the girl with the braces who once threw up in the middle of a geography lesson.

'Not much,' says her old schoolmate. 'How about you?'

'Well,' says Andrea, 'I was thinking of going to Thailand in October.'

Her old schoolmate, who isn't really sure where Thailand is and who knows nothing about Charlie and his double fracture (or about Andrea and her relationship with debt, come to that), becomes excited. 'Cor!' she says. 'If I were you I'd definitely go! Thailand! You'll have a ball!'

Andrea starts to mumble something about her bank manager and how bored stuntmen get when they're forced to stay in bed for weeks on end, but her old schoolmate waves aside these minor objections. 'Thailand in autumn!' she sighs. 'It's like in a song, isn't it? Oh, Angela,' she says, 'you absolutely have to go!'

As soon as she gets off the bus, Andrea heads straight for the travel agent's and books her flight. 'Everyone says I should go,' she informs the travel agent.

When Andrea returns from Thailand, having spent the entire two weeks under an umbrella eating wet rice, she discovers that Charlie has married his physio therapist during her absence. Andrea is devastated. How could he do this to her? Why did he let her go? Why did her friends and family let her go?

'You mean she doesn't feel responsible? She doesn't feel any guilt or remorse?'

Not a bit. It isn't Andrea's fault. It's everyone else's.

'But how can that be?' you query.

'I never wanted to go in the first place,' says Andrea. 'It was everyone else who talked me into it.'

Decisions

Every day of our lives, we are faced with hundreds of decisions to be made. Red socks or blue socks? Cornflakes or toast? Cornflakes *and* toast? Car, bus, bike or tube? Umbrella? Knowing this – and knowing, as well, that practice makes perfect – the casual student of human behaviour would be forgiven for assuming that most people take decision-making in their stride. Forgiven but wrong. And another point. If you can't make up your mind, you know it's because you're a thoughtful, sensitive and considerate individual. If, however, it's the other person, it's just downright annoying.

'What would you like to do, Anne?'

Anne shrugs. 'Oh, I don't know. Whatever you want to do.'

'No, no, it's your birthday. You decide.'

Anne shrugs again. 'Heavens, I don't know. What would you like to do?'

'Anne, it's your birthday. You have to choose what we do and where we go.'

Anne smiles wanly. 'Do you want to go out to eat?'

'If you do.'

Anne's smile becomes a little hopeful. 'Where would you like to eat?'

'No, Anne, you choose the restaurant.'

'Do you like Italian food?'

'Sure, Italian food's great.'

'You like Italian food better than Chinese food?'

'I like them both.'

Anne pushes her luck. 'How about Spanish food? Do you like Spanish food?'

'Yes. Spanish food's good, too.'

'Better than Chinese?'

'Anne, I like them all. *What* do you prefer?'

'Of course, we don't *have* to eat. We could go to a film instead.'

'Yes, we could do that.'

'Or we could do both, I suppose.'

'Both might be nice.'

'If we do both, which should we do first? Do you want to eat before we go to the cinema, or after?'

'Whatever you'd prefer.'

'What sort of film would you like to see?'

'It's your birthday, you choose . . .'

Deadlines

It can be supposed that the literal translation of the word 'deadline' means the point beyond which you are dead. And yet for all the seriousness with which many people take 'deadlines' they might as well be defined as 'the arbitrary date or time, after which someone might be grateful to receive something from you'.

What happens, exactly, when a person is given a deadline?

Let's say that P is given a deadline of 2 October. He is given this deadline on 16 September.

What does P do next?

Nothing. Well, not nothing exactly. He starts worrying about the deadline. Maybe he should have demanded a date in the middle of October. Maybe he's overextended himself. He goes over the work to be done. He sighs. He complains to his friends. 'Can you believe it?' he says. 'A deadline of 2 October.'

Then what does P do?

P continues to do nothing for a week. But every day he thinks about that deadline. Lord help us, how is he ever going to make it? Sixteen days is not enough time to do all he has to do. What do people think he is, some sort of miracle worker? He is baffled, truly, truly baffled.

Now what?

Nothing for a few days. He is so upset and puzzled over the little time given to him for the deadline that he can't get himself to sit down and do anything at first. 'This really is a pisser,' he tells strangers on the street. 'Sixteen days! That's all!'

And then?

On the evening of 1 October, P starts to work.

'And he makes the deadline anyway!' you exclaim. 'Isn't that something?'

No, he doesn't make the deadline. It takes him sixteen days to meet the deadline. That's why he was given sixteen days in the first place.

But it is not, of course, his fault that he didn't meet the deadline. He always knew it wasn't enough time. He always said the middle of October was much more realistic.

Anger

Get in touch with your emotions is one of the great catch-phrases of the twentieth century. And anger, obviously, is an important emotion, and one we should all be in touch with.

And yet some of us prefer to seethe in silence than lay our hands on our fury and throw it into the room where everyone else can see it.

You come home one evening, like any evening, you chuck your jacket over the jacket chair and toss your hat on top of the three shrunken oranges in the fruit bowl, and you call out, 'Hi, honey, I'm home!'

No answer.

You follow the sounds of human voices into the sitting-room, where honey is sitting in front of the television with the expression of someone in a hypnotic trance. 'Hi, honey,' you say. 'Have a good day?'

Honey's eyes don't move from the chocolate commercial. Honey's breathing is heavy.

Maybe honey hasn't heard you. 'Honey,' you say. 'Hi! I'm home!'

'Oh, is that you?' says honey, eyes now on the ad for pasta sauce. 'I thought it was the Queen.'

This sarcasm isn't totally lost on you. 'Honey,' you say, sitting down beside him on the sofa. 'Honey, is something wrong?'

'Wrong?' says honey, suddenly smiling at the dancing cows of the butter commercial. 'No, nothing's wrong.'

'Are you sure?' you ask.

'Of course I'm sure,' says honey.

'Really?' you say. 'You seem a little angry.'

'Angry?' honey repeats. 'Why should I be angry?'

'I don't know why you should be angry,' you say. 'But you seem a little . . .'

Honey's eyes meet yours. 'A little what?' asks honey sweetly.

Options scamper through your mind. Distant. Cold. Pissed off.

Furious. On the brink of suing for divorce. You choose one. 'Well
. . . um . . . tired?' you guess. 'Are you a little tired, honey?'

'No,' replies honey, going back to look at the screen, 'no, I'm not
tired.'

'And you're not . . . um . . . angry about anything?'

'No, I'm not angry.'

'And nothing's wrong?'

'Nothing's wrong.'

'What about dinner, then?' you ask pleasantly.

The set pops off. The remote control bounces across the carpet.
Honey is on his feet and halfway across the sitting-room before you
can say 'repressed emotions'.

'Get your own bloody dinner!' roars honey. 'I'm going out.'

If, months later, you happen to ask honey what he was angry about
that night, there is a ninety per cent chance that he will say. 'Angry?
What are you talking about? I wasn't angry.'

And a ten per cent chance that he will punch you on the nose.

Leaving Your Lover

It seems simple enough on the surface, doesn't it? You and C were
madly in love for several months or several years, and moderately fond
of one another for another block of time, but now you're not. Or one
of you is not. All it takes is for one of you to turn to the other and say,
'I'm terribly sorry about this, you know how much I like and respect
you, but I'm afraid the thrill is gone. Let's part as friends, though,
shall we?'

But instead what do we do?

Nothing.

Doing nothing is the most popular form of breaking up a relationship in the Western world. It's inexpensive, it doesn't take a lot of
effort, and it saves on the arguments about who gets the stereo and
who gets the microwave. It isn't as quick, perhaps, as pushing your
ex-beloved into a closet and stealing the car, but in the end it is just as
effective.

The negative side of doing nothing is that it annoys your friends.
They listen to your trials and tribulations, they stick up for you
whenever they find themselves in the middle of a fight (which is more

and more often as the years go on), they give you a place to stay on those nights when you can't stand it anymore. And what happens? Nothing.

'I don't understand,' say your friends. 'Why don't you just leave?'

'I would,' you say, 'but the cat's so fond of A. As soon as the cat gets over her illness, I'm moving out.'

'The cat seems fine now,' your friends point out. 'Why haven't you left yet?'

'A bought her her own little bed when she came back from the animal hospital. I couldn't leave after that. I'll have to wait till the cat dies.'

'So,' say your friends. 'The cat's dead. When's the big day?'

'But A's distraught over the cat's demise,' you say. 'As soon as A's recovered from that, I'm on my way.'

'What's *that*?' ask your friends, sounding just a wee bit churlish.

'Isn't it the cutest little kitten you ever saw?' you say. 'A bought it for me, to replace the cat.'

Behave badly.

Behaving badly is the second-most popular way of breaking up a relationship in the Western world. Behaving badly is similar to doing nothing, in that you yourself don't directly do anything to end things, you wait for your partner to get fed up enough to do it for you.

'So what sort of bad behaviour are we talking about here? Poisoning the dog? Inviting a family of refugees to sleep in the sitting-room?'

Either of those things might, of course, work, but bad behaviourists seldom have that sort of imagination. Nor do they want to run the risk that the person they live with is one of the millions who can happily become accustomed to half a dozen Hungarians drinking borscht in the sitting-room. What they want is something that's guaranteed to annoy.

'You mean like an affair.'

The tackier the better. A relative or close friend of the ex-beloved is usually a good choice. Or someone the ex-beloved loathes.

'But what if your partner doesn't find out?'

As long as the adulterer wants the partner to find out, the partner will find out. He will begin to notice that the karate lessons last a little longer each week. She will find the journal where he's written down all the details. He will notice that she has developed an interest in Czechoslovakian films. She'll find someone else's earring in the salad crisper. He'll come across that photograph on her bulletin board. There will be a teary confession at three in the morning after a fight about how one should or should not wrap up the rubbish.

'It sounds pretty foolproof.'

Yes and no. In order for it to work, you have to bank on the fact that your partner isn't going to do nothing. Or, worse yet, behave badly as well.

Divorce

The day a couple becomes legally separated, as my grandmother in all her wisdom once told me, is not the end of the marriage; it's the beginning of the divorce. 'You never really know a person until you divorce them,' my grandmother also said. 'If you thought they were crazy when you liked each other, just wait till you try living apart.'

Dividing the Property

'Eventually,' said Lisa, 'we had to get our solicitors to go through the house and draw up a list of everything we owned, put each item on a separate piece of paper, put it all into a hat, and then we took turns choosing.'

'Sort of like a lucky dip,' I said.

She wrinkled her nose. 'Sort of. More dip than lucky, if you ask me.'

'Um,' I said. 'Why did you have to do it this way? I mean, you and Barry had quite an amicable divorce, didn't you? Couldn't you have just, you know, worked it out between you?'

Lisa smiled grimly. 'We tried that,' she said. 'Fourteen times, if you want to know the truth. One time he threw the stereo out of the bedroom window because I said I considered it mine since I had paid for it.'

'Out of the window? Barry? But he's such a gentle guy.'

'Goes to show you, doesn't it?' smirked Lisa. 'He said it was his because I gave it to him as a Christmas present.'

'Oh.'

'I said in that case I was keeping the car, since that had been a birthday present. More or less.'

'Well,' I said, 'I guess I can see why you had to resort to the lawyers.'

'Then another time I went for him with the silver teapot his grandmother gave us for our wedding.'

'Went for him?'

'He made some crack about my cooking that just made me wild. You know, about how I didn't really need the stainless steelware as I did most of my cooking in the microwave anyway? So I threw the teapot at him.'

'Phew,' said I. 'That teapot was heavy. It's lucky you missed.'

'I didn't miss,' said Lisa, sounding surprised. 'I concussed him.'

'Remember when you and Barry were so in love?' I gasped. 'Remember when he was the finest man who ever lived?'

'No,' said Lisa. 'I don't think I do. All I remember is the way he always corrected me when I was in the middle of a story.'

'So who got the dishes?' I joked.

'No one,' said Lisa. 'We smashed them all the third time we tried to divide the property. You know that soup tureen you loved so much?' I nodded. 'It landed in a million pieces in the bath tub.'

'Well,' I said. 'I guess it was good that you did do a lucky dip in the end.'

Lisa shrugged. 'It didn't really matter all that much by then,' she said. 'There wasn't that much left.'

'Your and Barry's record collection?' I whispered.

'Oh that,' said Lisa. She shrugged again. 'He got the stove in the lucky dip, so I baked all his albums in it.'

I held up my hand. 'Wait a minute,' I said. 'You mean even though it was a fair and equal draw, you took retribution?'

'Whose side are you on?' snapped Lisa. 'Barry's? Well don't go feeling sorry for Barry. You should have seen the way he carried on when I drew the leather sofa. You know what a thing he had about that leather sofa.'

'Didn't his grandfather bring it over from Russia on a raft?' I asked.

'That's beside the point,' said Lisa. 'It was communal property. He had no right to attack my solicitor like that.'

'*Barry?* Barry the five-foot-four glass blower *attacked* your solicitor?'

'He said the dip was fixed.'

'Barry?'

'Did I tell you that he threw all my underwear over the lawn, too?' asked Lisa. She smirked grimly. 'See if you can defend that,' she said.

Dreams of the Divorced

'I don't know what came over me,' said Barry. 'One minute I was sitting in McDonalds with the kids, and the next minute I was driving to the ferry, telling them how much they were going to enjoy living in France.'

'I suppose you must have missed them,' I said. 'I mean the kids, not the ferries.'

'Oh, yes, of course,' said Barry. 'But it wasn't that. It was because of my dream.'

In Barry's dream, Lisa, his ex-wife, started dating. Barry could take that, that Lisa was going to start dating other men, of course he could, he was a mature and sensitive human being, and he and Lisa had been divorced for several years by then. He'd been dating, it was only natural that Lisa would, too. But in the dream it wasn't just that Lisa was dating. She was telling him what her dates were like. He'd dream that he was in the office, or maybe lunching with a client, and suddenly Lisa would appear. 'You should've seen the hunk I was out with last night,' she'd say. She'd roll her eyes. 'I told him all about how you would never make love anywhere except the bed and he said I was obviously sexually deprived. He said you sounded incurably repressed to him.' She'd sit down. She'd start laughing. She'd turn to whoever else was present and start talking to them. She'd tell them everything she and the man she was dating did together. She'd nod towards Barry. 'Thank God,' she'd say, 'this guy's got a smaller tongue than old Barry here, but his penis is just enormous!'

'Wow,' I mumbled. 'Some dream. So how did that get you halfway to Chartres?'

'The kids said Lisa had a boyfriend. They said he was at least six foot tall. All I could think of was the two of them laughing at me in my own bed.'

'But it's not your bed,' I pointed out. 'You axed your bed when you and Lisa were dividing the property.'

'I meant figuratively,' said Barry.

'So you kidnapped the kids,' I said.

'It was an awful dream,' said Barry.

Eight Years after the Divorce

Eight years after the divorce, Barry started dating Lisa's best friend. Lisa, by then, had remarried and had had another child. She was madly in love with her new husband, and he with her. She was happier than she'd ever been. And then what happened? Barry started going out with Judith.

Lisa called me in tears. 'I can't believe this!' she screamed. 'What a bitch!'

I said, 'Excuse me? Who's a bitch?'

'Oh, don't *you* start!' roared Lisa. 'You know perfectly well who I'm talking about. That Judas in dyed-blonde hair, Judith Blythe.'

I said, 'Excuse me, Lisa, but wasn't Judith the person who helped and supported you all through your divorce? Didn't you say if it weren't for her you would have had a complete breakdown?'

'Hurumph!' said Lisa, or a sound to that effect. 'Now we know why Judith was so nice to me.'

'Why?'

'So she could date my husband behind my back!'

'But he's not your husband and it's not behind your back.'

Lisa started sobbing even louder. 'She'd planned this all along,' she shrieked. 'This is the only reason she ever made friends with me, so she could go out with Barry.'

I said, 'What?'

'You heard me,' Lisa screamed. 'She only pretended to be my best friend so she could go out with my husband.'

'But Barry's not your husband,' I said faintly. 'Leon is.'

'All of it,' wailed Lisa. 'The overnight parties, the holidays, the coffee mornings, the time she went with me to get the pill. It was just part of her scheme to get my defences down.'

'Uh,' I said. 'Uh, Lisa. You can't be serious. You and Judith met in kindergarten. You can't honestly believe that she engineered that just so thirty-two years later she could go out with Barry?'

'I wouldn't put anything past that bitch,' said Lisa.

60

THEY'RE OUT TO GET YOU

Alone

You are well-balanced, mature and adult. You have gone through all the rites of passage that the twentieth century can provide and you have survived each one. No, you haven't just survived, you have flourished. You've been away to university. You've travelled through Europe (two weeks on an under-thirties tour). You've changed jobs three times. You've moved house twice. There are no challenges life can offer that you won't face with intelligence and dignity.

How about being alone?

'Alone?' you say, a slight smile playing at the corners of your mouth. 'What do you mean "alone"?'

I mean alone, as in By Yourself.

The smile deepens. 'Don't be ridiculous,' you say. 'I'm alone all the time!'

Really? When was the last time you were alone?

'I was alone for two days last summer when my wife took the kids to her mother's.'

Most people do not like to be alone. They will do anything they can to avoid it. Work late every night and go into the office on weekends. Invent the video machine. Take a night course in Sanskrit. Give dinner parties. Stay married to someone they can't stand because the alternative – not being married to anyone – is so much more ghastly than the thought of spending the next twenty-five years with someone they wish they'd never met.

'Oh, come on,' you say. 'I just told you. I'm alone all the time.'

Two days during August while the rest of the family goes to Bognor to visit a woman who once fed you dogfood to discourage you from marrying her daughter isn't too bad. You can usually find someone to go to the cinema with you one of those nights, and someone to go out for a meal with the other. If you can't, there's usually something to do in the house that you've been putting off tackling for the past four years (the shelves you started building the last time your wife took the kids to her mother's, for instance).

But what if you are alone all the time?

'All the time?'

Uh huh. Let's not even talk about for ever, let's say you're alone for a month. Maybe two months. The days are all right, because you're at work. But what about the nights? That's roughly sixty nights that have to be filled.

'Hmmm,' you frown. 'That's a lot of shelving.'

A lot of shelving and a lot of pizza and films, too. But you cannot, of course, go out every night. You cannot clean out the cupboards for sixty nights. You cannot have people over from Monday to Monday. At some point you're going to find yourself in the sitting-room, on your own, with nothing to do. The television will have shut down for the night. The video will be over. It'll be too late to call your mother and start a fight. What'll you do then?

'Go to sleep?'

But you can't sleep. You don't notice it when the house is filled with people, but all sorts of things go on in your home once the lights have been turned off. You're sure you can hear rats in the walls. And that groaning sound. Is that groaning sound a ghost, or is it the mains about to burst? And what about that sort of hum you hear in the attic? Are those carpenter ants, gnawing through the support beams? You start worrying about the boiler. It's been a while since you had it serviced. And what about your pension? Is your pension really going to be enough to support you comfortably in your old age? Something goes bang clink rattle in the kitchen. No, your pension is not going to be enough to support you even uncomfortably in your old age. You're going to become a bag person, that's what you're going to become. You're going to have to tie old newspapers around your feet in the winter to keep them from frostbite. Only there won't be any old newspapers because they're all being recycled. Your feet will fall off. You'll be dragging all your possessions (not that there will be many of those left by then, since you just realized that you don't have enough insurance in case of fire) around on your knees. Something falls with a thud in the garden. That's it, then. You don't have to worry about becoming a bag person or the house burning down, you're about to be murdered by a psychopath. You reach under your pillow for the can of air freshener and the garden trowel you hid there. If you lived in America you would have a submachine-gun under your pillow, but you don't live in America, you live in Britain, so a garden trowel and a tin of air freshener are the best you can do. Your heart pounding and your lungs hyperventilating, you tip-toe into the hallway. You walk into the wall. Catching your breath, you proceed towards the door to the garden. You step firmly in the cat-litter tray. Rubbing your foot on the leg of your pyjamas, you sneak up on the garden door. Yes, you can hear them; the soft but dangerous footsteps of a psychopath slowly approaching your home. With a monumental surge of courage, you suddenly push open the door, leap into the garden and spray Spring Bouquet air freshener all over your next-door neighbour while soundly whacking him on the head with the garden trowel. When the two of you recover enough to be able to speak you ask him what he was doing out in the garden at three in the morning in his pyjamas. 'Well,' he says, wincing in pain, 'the wife took the kids to her mother's for a few days, you know, and, well, I haven't been sleeping so well . . . and, well . . . I thought I heard something outside.'

Animals

Many of our problems with animals stem from a fear of being attacked by them. 'Well, that's reasonable,' you say. 'I've spent my life in fear of marauding rabbits since Bugs, our school bunny, mistook my finger for a carrot when I was nine.' Fair enough. Not all animal phobias, however, are of the fangs and claws variety.

Canine-on-Furniturephobia – fear of the dog getting on the sofa

My Aunt Beryl was so afraid that the dog would go up on the furniture when she was out of the house or sleeping, that she used to try to trick him. She had never actually caught him in the act, but she had seen an imprint on the sofa on more than one morning and found tell-tale dog hairs on the armchair. Knowing, however, that you can't discipline an animal unless you catch it doing what it's not supposed to do, she would put on her coat and her hat, pick up her bag, and call out, 'Well, I think I'll go into town for a few hours.' She would then march smartly out of the house and down the street in the direction of the bus stop. Once there, she would double back, tip-toe around to the back door, and, hiding her shoes, her purse, her coat and her hat in the rhododendrons, crawl through the pantry window. She would then proceed into the sitting-room on her hands and knees. Although Aunt Beryl was twice apprehended by the local constabulary, she never caught the dog on the sofa. And then she hit upon the perfect solution. She mined the sitting-room furniture with mousetraps.

'Mousetraps? Did it work?'

After a fashion. The mousetraps yielded two vicars, one solicitor and one mother-in-law.

'And the dog?'

He went right on sleeping on the furniture.

Authority

Many of us treat authority as we do fire. It's there, we appreciate that we need a certain amount of it, but we'd prefer that it didn't take over our homes. Basically, we fear and/or respect authority enough not to commit bigamy or turn up to cousin Charlotte's wedding in surfing shorts and running shoes; but we don't fear and/or respect it so much that we always drive within the speed limit or never fiddle our taxes.

That aside, it is possible, if you're so inclined, to divide people into two groups: 1. those who have a problem with authority; and 2. those who have a problem with authority.

The first group is made up of those whose first instinct upon being told to do something is never simply to do it. They either want to know why they should do it, and then disagree and do something else, or they immediately do something else. Small children, adolescents, and criminals tend to fall into this group. 'What?' they say. 'Why?' they ask. 'Says who?' they'd like to know. For these people, authority is something to be either flouted, challenged or unthinkingly ignored. Group one make lousy tour groups, poor soldiers, difficult offspring, troublesome students, terrific resistance leaders and excellent union negotiators.

The second group is comprised of those whose first instinct upon being told to do something is to do it. They panic if they find themselves inadvertently going up the down staircase. They never rip that DO NOT REMOVE tag from their mattresses. When told to jump, they ask, 'How far?' They aren't too good at making decisions.

These people have a ball on tours, love the military, are dutiful children, troublefree students, and, ironically, great mobs.

Oddly enough, the second instinct of people in this group is often not to do what they are told. But if they go with this instinct, they suffer for it. Unlike the members of group one, who reason that they have as much right to an opinion on how things are run as anyone else, the members of group two can never completely convince themselves of this. Incapable of actually flouting or ignoring authority, they slink around it. Guilt dogs them. Worry haunts their days.

'We wouldn't be talking about Bunny Hofstra, would we by any chance?'

As a matter of fact, we would.

I am reminded of the time Bunny's father, Eugene P. Hofstra, Sr, came to visit Bunny in Putney. No sooner was the visit announced, than Bunny collapsed on the sofa with his head in his hands. 'Now what am I going to do?' he moaned. 'My father's coming. He's going to be very upset.'

I had never met Bunny's father, nor heard much about him. 'Buy a mug that isn't chipped and a packet of biscuits?' I suggested.

Bunny shook his head. 'You don't understand,' said Bunny. 'My father's not going to be pleased. He has standards. He's a successful man. He's used to certain things.'

'Like what?' I inquired, intrigued.

'White walls,' mumbled Bunny, looking dolefuly around him at the electric-blue walls of the sitting-room. 'Daddy says that coloured walls are the mark of barbarians.'

'In this case,' I pointed out, 'they're the mark of someone who bought his paint on special offer.' I didn't know Bunny very well at that time, and had never known him not to at least smile at a joke.

But he wasn't smiling. He was continuing. 'And carpets,' he was saying. 'Daddy says only natives fail to put carpets on their floors.'

'Bunny,' I said, 'as a jazz drummer, you barely make enough money to feed yourself and pay the bills. How are you supposed to afford carpets?'

The blood fled from Bunny's face. A look of terror so pure and complete came over him that for a second I thought he might be having a heart attack. Or choking on something, though as he was neither eating nor drinking at the time it would have been hard to say on what.

'Bunny!' I screamed, trying to remember if you were supposed to thump choking victims on the chest or on the back, wondering if I should call an ambulance, or if I should wait to see if he died, since I wouldn't want to call an ambulance and then discover that there was actually nothing wrong with him.

'Shhhhhhhh!!!' hissed Bunny. 'Don't say that so loud!'

I was afraid I might have inadvertently expressed my confusion about mouth-to-mouth resuscitation – were you meant to hold the nose closed or not? 'Say what?'

'Jazz drummer.'

I looked around. We were alone, in a flat off the Upper Richmond Road, at three o'clock in the afternoon. Who did he think was listening? 'Why not? It's not an illegal profession, is it?'

'To my father it is,' said Bunny, *sotto voce*.

'Let me get this straight,' I said, 'are you telling me that your father doesn't *know* you're a musician?'

Too stricken to speak, Bunny nodded dumbly.

'Well, if your father doesn't know that you're a musician, what is it he thinks you do?'

Bunny looked at me bleakly. 'Tax law,' he whispered.

It was true, I remembered, Bunny had qualified as a solicitor. But as soon as he'd arrived in London, he had abandoned conveyancing for the thumpthumpthump of his favourite percussion instrument.

'But where would he get an idea like that?' I asked. The bleak look remained fixed. 'From *you*?' I ventured. Bunny nodded, also bleakly. 'But Bunny,' I protested, 'why did you let him believe you were still in law?'

'It's what he's always wanted for me,' bleated Bunny.

'But you hate it.'

'But he wants it.'

'Well,' I said, 'then this is the best things that could have happened, isn't it? Your father will come to London, find out that you are following your heart's passion by playing in Buddy's Club three nights a week, that you live in a blue flat and don't own one coffee mug that isn't chipped.'

Bunny passed out.

Bunny decided that there was more wrong with the flat than just the colour of the walls. It was too noisy; his father hated noise. It was four flights up. Eugene Hofstra Sr had always advised his children never to live at the top of the house because of the risk of falling chimneys. Bunny's father would not approve of the neighbourhood. There weren't enough cupboards. The fridge was too small.

Bunny moved.

That solved one problem, but not the other. Bunny borrowed a couple of suits from friends, brought the drums round to my place, and littered his new, white, many-cupboarded flat with copies of *Law Today*, the *Financial Times*, and *Taxes: The Last Frontier*. He bought coffee cups. He bought coffee. He took out a loan. He bought a coffee maker. He bought a carpet. He came back to my place, and took the drums and sold them, because he was sure his father would *know* about them if he didn't. He used the money from the drums to buy a computer. His father approved of high technology.

And was his father fooled? Did the white walls and the dark suits make him happy?

His father never came. Something else came up that he had to do that day.

Reactions to the News that Your Boss Would Like to Talk to You

The boss wants to see me? I wonder why?

Hey, I know, I bet she's going to give me that rise I put in for.

That's it, it must be the rise. What else could it be? I haven't done anything wrong.

Have I?

It couldn't be about that little oversight with the fax to Norway could it?

Why would she be upset about that? It was all right in the end, wasn't it?

Was it?

Well, even if it wasn't, it's the sort of thing that could happen to anyone.

Isn't it?

But it didn't happen to anyone, it happened to me.

If she found about Norway, maybe she found out who burned out the photocopier last month.

She wouldn't fire you for that. The photocopier must be insured.

That doesn't mean she wanted it to explode.

It was an accident. It could have happened to anyone.

But it didn't happen to anyone, it happened to me.

It would have self-destructed for someone else if it hadn't been you, it was just bad luck that you were using it at the time.

But I wasn't even copying company papers. I was running off invitations to my daughter's birthday party.

Everybody runs off invitations to their daughters' birthday parties on the office copier.

Perhaps someone found out about my little indiscretion with the photocopier mechanic?

Maybe I should just quit now and save myself the humiliation of being thrown out on my ear.

Extramarital Affairs

What does it feel like to be having an affair? Exciting? Thrilling? Rejuvenating? Well, that's what it's *supposed* to feel like. But what if you're of a slightly jittery disposition?

Every Friday evening at 8.30 Lionel Elwood, dressed in his old work pants, his flannel shirt and his oiled jacket, his hip boots under his arm and his fishing pole over his shoulder, kissed his wife and children goodbye and went off to spend the weekend fishing. Fishing was his passion. 'I knew when I married him that I'd have to share him with fresh-water trout,' Mrs Elwood often joked.

What she didn't know, of course, was that in actuality she was sharing him with Kimberley Winnesota. Every Friday, dressed like someone out of *Field and Stream*, Lionel went not to the cottage in the country with his cronies but five miles away to the small but dry flat that belonged to Kimberley. If people in her building thought it odd that she was visited at the weekends by a fisherman – that is, if they wondered whether or not she had a river coursing through her sitting-room – they never said anything.

'But wait a minute,' you say. 'What happened when he went back home on Sunday without any fish?'

He didn't. On Saturday morning, disguised as a KGB agent in a grey overcoat and brown fedora, pulled low (just in case, for some unexplained reason, his wife had stopped shopping in Sainsbury's and switched to the market instead), Lionel would go and buy fish. After he bought the fish, he would sit in the car and eat the breakfast his wife always made for him so he could get an early start on Saturday morning.

'Why did he eat it in the car?'

Because Kimberley was jealous of Mrs Elwood and wouldn't let Lionel eat food his wife had prepared for him in her house.

'Why didn't he just throw it away in Kimberley's dustbin?'

Because Kimberley was really jealous of Mrs Elwood. She didn't like to even hear her name mentioned, let alone have her sandwiches festering in her dustbin.

'So why didn't he just throw it in the bin outside?'

Abject and irrational terror. He once did just that, but as soon as he was back in Kimberley's flat, he became convinced that his wife was walking on the street outside. He could imagine her thinking to herself that morning, *Why don't the kids and I drive five miles away to a section of town we've never been to and take a walk, it's such a nice day?* Kimberley was telling him how much she had missed him that week, but all he could hear was his wife saying, 'Wait a minute darlings, I just want to look in this dustbin.' A cold sweat trickling down his back, he returned outdoors, dug around in the rubbish, and buried his breakfast under several leaking black bags and a wadge of disposable nappies. Then he went back inside. He closed his eyes to passionately embrace his mistress, but the image of his wife, chucking disposable nappies into the front garden and exclaiming, 'Why, those are the cheese sandwiches I made for Lionel!' took a bit of the thrill from it. He went back outside, dug through the rubbish again, and threw his breakfast in the bin of the people at the end of the road. He and Kimberley were just sitting down to enjoy a champagne lunch when it occurred to him that his wife would recognize the sandwiches as his, no matter whose dustbin they were in. If she discovered them at the end of the road she would ring every bell until she'd found him. The whole of Chesterfield Drive would know about him and Kimberley. That was approximately 300 people. Three hundred people he didn't know, but whom he would immediately run into after that everywhere he went. He got into the car and drove the sandwiches (and the fruit and the packet of biscuits) to Oxford, a town his wife never visited. He lay awake half the night, worrying that his wife had decided to go to Oxford that day.

'He must have been happy when dawn finally broke.'

When dawn finally broke he was in Oxford, going through some stranger's dustbin, looking for his breakfast.

'Is there a lesson to be learned in this?'

Yes.

Love makes you insane.

Jealousy

'Where has your brother gone?' I asked.

Sophie's brother was in town on business overnight and we were having dinner with him. We'd met him at his hotel and had only just arrived at the restaurant.

'He had to phone home,' said Sophie.

'Phone home?' I repeated. 'But he phoned home before we left the hotel. Unless, of course he has more than one home, like your Uncle Shep.'

Sophie shook her head. 'No, Jack's only got the one.'

I looked over to where Jack was standing beside a waiter. The waiter was talking on the phone, Jack just seemed to be standing there, looking pained. 'How strange,' I said, a comment Sophie was accustomed to hearing me make. 'You'd almost think the waiter was talking to Jack's wife.'

Sophie picked up a bread roll and began to crumble it. 'He is,' she said simply.

'He is what?'

'He is talking to Jack's wife.'

I acquired a bread roll of my own. 'Does he know her?'

Sophie shook her head. 'No.'

'Well, what's he saying to her?'

'He's telling her that Jack really is in Gino's Trattoria with the women in the picture.'

'What picture?'

'The picture of you and me in front of Shakespeare's statue!'

'Sophie!' I hissed. 'I told you to burn that picture!'

'I can't burn that picture,' snapped Sophie. 'It's the only one of me that doesn't make me look as though I've been somebody's beginner's taxidermy project.'

'You could at least have cut me out of it.'

Sophie pointed her roll at me. 'If I had you wouldn't have been able to meet my brother tonight, because he wouldn't have been able to prove you were a friend of mine and not his mistress.'

'Excuse me?'

Sophie explained. Jack's wife was convinced that he was having an affair. There was no reason for her to think this, Jack claimed, she just did. 'Jack thinks she's bored,' said Sophie. 'Now that the kids are all in school . . .'

'Why doesn't she get a job?' I inquired. After her children were all in school, my mother became a fanatical housekeeper. You couldn't breathe near a mirror because she'd immediately polish it. You had to take your shoes off not before you entered the house, but before you entered the driveway, as she swept that too. She put plastic on everything. It was like living in a sandwich bag. Eventually, she was persuaded to take up knitting. She knitted small animals. You couldn't eat at the kitchen table anymore, because it was covered with mice and squirrels in pastel hues. But it was preferable to being scolded if you left fingerprints on the taps.

'She can't get a job,' said Sophie. 'Jack works at home.'

'Yes?'

'If she's out of the house, who will monitor his phonecalls?'

'You mean she listens in on his phonecalls?'

'It's sort of eerie,' said Sophie. 'You'll be talking away for several minutes, and all of a sudden he'll say, "Helena? Helena, I'm on the phone", and she'll either hang up or she'll say she wanted to call the butcher or something.' Sophie shrugged in a puzzled, thoughtful way. 'It's not as though you're ever talking about anything important,' she went on, 'but it makes you feel weird. Like MI5's listening in on your conversation with your mother.'

'She does this a lot?'

'All the time. That's why she can't get a job. It would interfere.'

Over at the telephone, the bartender was joining Jack and the waiter. Jack handed the bartender the receiver. The bartender started shaking his head.

'Wait a minute,' I said. 'Surely Helena must realize that it's pointless to listen in on every phone conversation Jack has. If he were having an affair, he wouldn't have his lover call him at home because he knows his wife listens in on all his calls.'

73

'Yes, but Helena thinks that if she didn't he would.'

'You mean if she wasn't there to listen in on his calls, his lover would call him at home?'

'Exactly.'

'And she lets him out of the house?'

'He has to go out sometimes, doesn't he?' asked Sophie. 'There's his business, and taking the car to the garage, and shopping, and going places with the kids, and he plays squash and does a night class in Italian.'

A waitress had joined Jack, the waiter, and the bartender at the phone. She was talking to Helena with a very earnest expression on her face.

I crumbled my breadroll in an awestruck way. 'How does she handle that, I mean, maybe he isn't going to Italian lessons. Maybe he's meeting his girlfriend.'

'Helena and the kids drive him to his classes and pick him up again.'

'Men have been known to sneak in one door and right out the other.'

'She gives him an arbitrary amount of time – maybe fifteen minutes, maybe forty – and then she walks past the room, just to make sure that he's in there and the teacher really is Mr Fantelli.'

'He doesn't go fishing, does he?' I asked.

Sophie said no. Jack used to enjoy fishing, but it's not as much fun when you've got a woman who hates fishing, three children who hate fishing, two cats who are indifferent to it, and a dog who likes to swim with you.

'But what about business lunches and squash games and running into town for a packet of biscuits and a pint of milk? Surely there's scope in there for a few hot hugs in the back of the BMW.'

'She times him.'

Sophie and I both reached for another roll. I contemplated eating this one. 'She times him?'

'Uh huh. She knows how long it takes to get into town and find a parking place and go back because you thought you forgot to lock the car and pick up the shopping. And how long it takes to get to and from the squash courts and play a game.'

'What if he's late?'

'He tries not to be.'

Jack was handing the phone to a fellow diner. The waiter was passing around glasses of wine and a plate of olives. The crowd at the phone looked like it was having a pretty good time. They were certainly getting better service than we.

'I'm amazed she doesn't follow him.'

Sophie nibbled her roll. 'She only does that once a month or so,' she informed me. 'You know, like spot inspections in the army. You never know when one will happen so you always have to be ready.'

'So, let me get this straight,' I said. 'When he goes out of town, he has to phone her wherever he goes to prove that he's actually where he says he is?'

Sophie nodded.

'That's why there are half a dozen people at the telephone, talking to Jack's wife.'

'Precisely.'

'But what if they're all lying? What if he's really at a party at his girlfriend's and he's only pretending to be out of town?'

'Now that she knows where he is, she'll call back in half an hour and speak to the manager.'

'And this is all because she's bored?'

'And because she loves him so much,' said Sophie. 'Love . . . boredom . . . it's hard to tell them apart sometimes.'

Overhearing

You are entering a gala party being held in your honour, one of the most beautiful women in the world on your arm. You have just won an award for doing something terribly nice for an endangered breed of South American killer eagle that no one else likes, and you are about to be presented to the Queen. This is your night. You have never felt so together, so confident, so secure. Talk about having your pearl in your oyster! Your oyster's just about pissing pearls.

And then, as you pass into the main room, one of the most beautiful women in the world, the one getting foundation on the shoulder of your tuxedo, starts telling you another anecdote about her mother. At that exact moment, you hear, out of one ear, someone quite near you say in a harsh whisper to someone else, 'Cor, and they think the Prince has big ears.'

The universe implodes around you. Your blood becomes an arctic stream. Your pearls are sucked into the chasm of space. Big ears? You? You wish that one of the most beautiful women in the world would shut up about how her mother never gave her any compliments when she was little, because you want to make sure that you heard right. You tilt to the left. The words 'enormous' and 'regular Dumbo' scurry through the party chatter. You're sure you hear tittering and someone sigh, 'I'd rather be homeless than look like that.' Your eyes dart towards the direction of the Greek chorus. Everyone's smiling. At you. No, not smiling, laughing. They are pretending to smile – politely, pleasantly, engagingly even – but in reality they are nearly hysterical with mirth. And in that instant you realize that this is the way it has always been. You thought people were smiling at you because they liked you, because you were interesting, because you befriended unpopular species, but the terrible truth is that they were smiling to keep from losing their teeth through laughter. You turn back to one of the most beautiful women in the world (who is probably also legally blind but too vain to wear glasses and so hasn't noticed your ears). She is recounting an argument she had with her mother when she was thirteen and her mother made her change her clothes because she looked like a tramp. You, as it happens, don't know that that is what she is talking about. You are barely aware that she is speaking, how can you be expected to actually absorb what she's saying as well? And anyway, if the truth be told, she's been banging on about her mother for hours, and you're getting pretty tired of it. Maternal treatment is not what's at issue here. What's at issue is the devastating news that you have big ears! Great, enormous wings for ears! Your date gives you a little nudge in the ribs.

'Are you listening to me?' she demands.

Your lips move into a smile position. 'Of course I am, darling,' you say. You can say this so smoothly because you can't see her. All you can see are a thousand moments from your life when you, hatless and innocent, paraded around the world with your ears flapping in the breeze like flags. When you, thinking yourself just like everyone else, walked through crowds, stood before cameras, addressed rapt audiences, unaware that the whole time the one thought in everybody's head was: *Good God! How does he keep from falling over?*

'Well?' asks your date. 'Don't you think that's diabolical? Imagine, no new shoes for six months. How could a mother do that to her own child?'

You stare into her no-adjective-too-excessive gorgeous face. You're sure you hear someone whisper 'beast'. They're comparing the two of you to beauty and the beast. No prizes for guessing which is which. 'At least he was a millionaire,' someone else whispers. They're not comparing you to beauty and the beast, they're comparing you to Jackie and Onassis. Have you shrunk as well?

'You aren't listening to me!' your date complains. 'Are you? You haven't listened to a word I said.'

But you don't hear her, because you're halfway to the men's room. You hurl yourself at the mirror. You stare at your reflection. Your ears look exactly as they have always looked. Which is not too large. But obviously they are too large, you can see that now. Why did you never notice that before? Why did no one ever mention it? Not even in primary school? How did they let you get away with it? They could have made your life hell. Someone must have paid the little buggers off. You race back to the cloakroom where there's a phone. You call your mother. 'I don't believe this!' you shout at her. 'Why did you never tell me the truth? How could you keep it a secret for so long?'

Your mother sighs. 'Now what have I done?' she asks. She turns to speak to someone in the room with her, probably her sister, they're thick as thieves, those two. 'It's always my fault,' she says. 'I take the blame for everything.'

Depression

Everyone gets depressed now and then. Why shouldn't we get depressed? The dolphins are dying. There's a hole in the sky. Warren and Madonna have broken up. If cryonics is perfected, we'll probably never get rid of Richard Nixon.

But there is depression – that bad mood that hits you after a hard week, when you push the dog around and slam doors and eat every biscuit in the house and even drink the cooking sherry.

And there is depression.

My cousin, Scott, has been depressed since 1972, the year his marriage broke up, he lost his job, and he was forced to acknowledge that the Beatles had really split up for good. Being depressed for that many years is no easy thing, let me tell you.

Firstly, you have to get the voice right. You want people to know that you're suffering, but you don't want them to know that you never plan to stop suffering. It should be low and flat, but not too low or too flat or people will hang up on you immediately. If you get the right pitch, somewhere between abject despair and a bit under the weather, even after two decades of depression friends will still speak to you because they think maybe today's the day you're going to feel a little better.

Secondly, you must become extraordinarily skilled at avoiding the fact that other people have problems, too, and at stomping on hope. This requires a great deal of tenacity and determination, the human spirit being what it is.

So, for instance, you call up Scott to see how he is, even though you know how he is, he is lousy. 'Hi, Scott,' you say, 'How are you?'

Scott sighs. 'I have a cold,' says Scott.

'It's the weather,' you say. 'Everyone I know has a cold. Maweena just got over bronchial pneumonia.'

'I've had this cold for two weeks,' says Scott. 'And I got caught in that rain this morning. Completely ruined a brand new pair of shoes.'

'At least we didn't have the blizzard they predicted,' you say.

'But the weathermen said nothing about the rain,' Scott persists. 'I depend on them so I'm prepared for the day, and what happens? They let me down!'

'You work too hard,' you say. 'You should get out and have a little fun.'

'Work too hard?' queries Scott. 'If I don't work hard, who will? No one will, that's who. The whole office would shut down if it weren't for me. But do they thank me? No, they don't thank me. They barely give me a livable wage. They promote all these twelve-year-olds over me. They never give me a bonus. They send me to Finland for the company, but they don't send me to France. Oh, no, of course not. Don't send Scott to France. Send him to Finland. Even the Finns don't want to be in Finland.'

You've heard the piece about Finland before. It lasts for sixty-one minutes and tends to be repetitive. You try to change the subject. 'Why don't you take a little holiday, Scott. You know you deserve one.'

'I can't,' says Scott. 'I can't afford a holiday. I'd have to get some-one to look after the dog, and I'd need a new suitcase, and I don't have any casual clothes. All I do is work so I don't really need any casual clothes, and prices are so high now, and anyway, the number of air crashes there've been lately, not to mention hijackings . . .'

'You don't have to go by plane,' you say. 'You don't even have to leave the country. You could go by car and take the dog with you.'

'The dog gets car sick,' says Scott. 'And the car's on its last legs. I'd probably have to buy a new car to go anywhere. And then the dog would be sick in it every hour or so, and where can you stay when you've got a Rottweiler with you? People are very funny about dogs.'

'Camping,' you say. 'You and Percy could go camping. You could rent a van, and you could go camping.'

'Sleep on the ground?' says Scott. 'You know how prone I am to colds.'

You'd think that anyone as depressed as Scott would try to do away with himself, wouldn't you?

'Yes,' you say, 'I would.'

He did contemplate it once, but he fell asleep halfway through the suicide note. That depressed him so much that he couldn't face it again.

Hypochondria

As you are getting ready for bed one night, you notice a bruise on your leg. 'Hmmm,' you say to the bathroom, 'I didn't notice that before, did you?' None of the other people in the bathroom at the time noticed it before either.

'I wonder how I got that?' you ask. No one knows. 'Did I bump into something?' Neither you nor the shower curtains recalls you bumping into anything. 'Did someone bump into me?'

'Got us,' say the several varieties of bandages, plasters, and ointments in the medicine cabinet. You shake your head.

'Oh, well,' you say philosophically, 'I suppose these things hap-pen, right?'

The fourteen different cold remedies also in the medicine cabinet say, 'Yes.'

But later, as you're drifting off to sleep, you remember something.

79

Or half remember something. These things don't *just happen*. Isn't easy bruising a sign? Old memories, slumbering since the last time you read through the medical journal, curious about the odd shape of your cranium, begin to stir. It is a sign. But of what? 'Getting hit,' you say out loud, laughing nervously.

'Something besides getting hit,' you tell yourself. You shake your head. You thump your pillow. You close your eyes again. You open them.

'Something bad,' you say into the darkness of the night.

'Don't be ridiculous,' you chide yourself, 'it probably isn't something bad. It's probably a sign of thin skin or rich blood or something like that.'

You close your eyes again. They snap open.

'It isn't something bad,' you say. 'It's something awful.' You lie awake all night, thinking of all the awful things it could be. By the time dawn breaks, there isn't a cell in your body that doesn't hurt. Not only do you have some nameless awful something, you have a cracked rib, two deformed toes, a ringing in your ears, and a headache that is almost certainly the first sign of a brain tumour. You can barely stagger out of bed to phone the doctor.

'Back again?' asks the doctor as, pale and strained looking, you shuffle into his surgery. 'What is it this time?'

Deciding not to trouble him at this moment with all the other things that are wrong with you, especially not after last time, you explain about the bruising. You show him your leg. He says, 'It looks to me as though you bumped into something.'

You don't want to put ideas into his head, and you remember the way he snapped at you the time you suggested that he didn't appreciate the complications that can arise from the common cold, but you can't help feeling that he is forgetting about the awful things bruising can be a sign of. 'Well,' you say, calmly and unhysterically, 'if I did, it must have been a very light bump because I don't remember it.'

The doctor leans towards you across the desk. 'Let me guess,' he says. 'You think this might be a symptom of something more serious.'

Your heart stops in its tracks. You're right! It is a symptom of something awful! 'Oh, no, no,' you say quickly. 'It's just that I do seem to get these bruises quite often, and I never remember –'

'You have a bruise. You bumped into something,' the doctor interrupts you. He smiles. 'If you don't remember, well, maybe you don't have a very good memory.'

All the way home the doctor's smile floats in your mind's eye, the way the Cheshire cat's smile kept floating in the air before Alice's eyes. What did he mean by that smile? It wasn't just a normal, everyday smile, it was significant. And then, just as your leg stops aching and your brain tumour seems to have gone quiet, you realize what that smile meant. *Senile dementia*.

Dentist

The card arrives in the post: Dear Mr/Mrs/Miss/Ms _____, It is time for your six-month dental examination. Please phone for an appointment.

Do you phone?

Not the first week. You like to give it a few days for the idea of going back to the dentist, *again*, to sort of grow on you. The second week, as luck would have it, you forget. You remember somewhere in the middle of the third week, but then you forget again. At the beginning of the fourth week you say to yourself, 'O K, this week I have got to ring the dentist for an appointment.' You nod. You feel so good about this decision that it is almost as though you *have* phoned. So you don't.

Sometime during the second month since the arrival of your check-up notice, you begin waking up with anxiety sweats. You feel a slight throbbing on the lower left side of your jaw. Last night when you brushed your teeth they bled. While the bus is stuck in traffic one morning, you strike up a conversation with a woman who has just had major dental surgery. While the traffic fumes build up around you and your boss looks from her watch to your desk, your new friend describes the ordeal she went through in immaculate detail. You wince at every touch of the knife and wrench of the extractors. 'There was blood everywhere,' she says. 'And the *pain*.' She shakes her head. 'The dentist himself, he said to me, "Mrs Marshall, I don't know how you did it. I've seen war heroes cry out for less than what you went through."' By the time you get to work your mouth is in agony. After that, it takes you over an hour to brush your teeth every night: three minutes to brush them, and eighty-seven to stare at your open mouth in the mirror. The third month passes.

You can't fall asleep at night, worrying about your teeth. You're sure that there is something catastrophically wrong with your teeth. Or your gums. Or both. You, who can't remember what you had for supper last Sunday, remember every dentist horror story you've ever heard, and several that you were never told. Mouths sewn together. Death in the chair. Drills going out of control. People having to be strapped down and sat on by several hygienists. And what about AIDS? Didn't you read somewhere that you can catch AIDS from the dentist? Any dentist? Even if you bring your own glass, is that any guarantee?

Then one day you call the dentist for an appointment. Just like that, out of the blue, because you just read an article about gum infection poisoning the bloodstream. 'It's taken you long enough,' snaps the receptionist. 'We sent you your reminder nearly six months ago.'

'Don't be ridiculous,' you snap back. 'It only just arrived.'

Birth Control

The Series

Episode One – The Condom

You have never bought a packet of condoms before, but you already know that you hate it. It's worse than buying any number of other intimate items, because with most things you can pretend that they're for someone else. 'This delouser's for my cousin who's visiting from the swamp,' you can confide to the assistant. But you can't do that with condoms. Nobody buys condoms that they aren't intending to use themselves, in one way or another.

You linger in the cold outside the chemist's for two or three hours, trying to give the impression that you are waiting for someone while in fact you are waiting for everyone but the shop assistant to leave the building. Two or three times the store empties and you dash in, but always before you can quite bring yourself to stroll up to the counter and make your selection someone else comes in. Because of this, you have purchased one jar of vitamin pills, one bottle of shampoo, two bars of soap, two tubes of toothpaste (on special offer) a packet of breath mints, and the assistant looks as though she thinks you're casing the place for a robbery.

Finally, just as feeling in your feet begins to go, the store empties. You dash in. You were hoping that the assistant would find something to do in the back or in another section while you made your choice, but it is clear that she wouldn't turn her back on you, never mind letting you out of her sight. She is standing approximately twenty-four inches from the condom display, with her lips pursed, her eyes narrowed, and her hand on the phone. You smile cheerily. You stop breathing. Sweat pours down your body. You march up to the condoms. Oh my God! You never thought of this. They come in different sizes. Well they would, wouldn't they? you think to yourself.

If you are buying these condoms to put on your own person, you may be relieved at this point to discover that there is no such size as Small. There is Large. There is Extra Large. And there is He-man. But no Small. On the other hand, you may not be so delighted to discover this. Does this mean that large is small? you may wonder. Or does this mean that large is large? If large is large, then are you the only male in the entire world who takes a small? If large is large and you don't think you are, will it be too big? If it's too big, is there any point in buying it? What if it's so big that the semen just swims right out? What if it falls off? What if it falls off while it's on the job? What if it falls off while cries of ecstasy are filling the room and you can't retrieve it? What if the love of your life has to spend the next year with a large honey-flavoured, rainbow-coloured condom inside her? What then?

If you are buying these condoms just in case tonight is the night that you and the love of your life are swept away by passion but you're worried that he might not have the foresight to have a packet on him (not to mention the fact that if he did have a packet on him you would then have to worry that he either thought you were easy or that he never left the house without them, neither option likely to increase your passion level significantly), you then have the problem of having no idea at all as to whether Large or Extra Large is called for. 'What is it?' you start muttering to yourself. 'Is it big hands or big feet? Or is it ears?'

Because you worry too much about the pill (How often *can* I forget it? What if I'm one of the small percentage of women the doctors say might develop complications? What if it isn't water retention, what if it really does make you fat?), and because you worry too much about the coil (What if they can't get it out? What if it gets stuck? What if it doesn't work? Remember that story about Molly Pickering's sister . . .), and because you worry about condoms (What if we've got a defective packet? What if large does mean large?), you get a diaphragm. All your friends say that the diaphragm is user friendly. It is efficient. It has no side effects. It works.

There are one or two things that your friends don't tell you, however.

They don't tell you that the day after you first use your diaphragm Molly Pickering will tell you another story about her sister. The pinhole story.

'Triplets,' Molly Pickering says with a sad shake of her head. 'Can you believe it?'

You can believe it.

'She doesn't even know how it could have happened,' says Molly Pickering. 'She always took care of it. She never just tossed it into a corner or anything.'

Well, you think, that's a relief.

'And yet that's how she got pregnant,' Molly Pickering bangs on. 'There was a teensy tiny pinhole in her diaphragm. It wasn't even visible to the naked eye.'

Not visible to the naked eye?

Molly Pickering shakes her head sadly again. 'I guess it just proves that you can't be too careful,' she says.

You're not too careful. Every time you use your diaphragm you spend twenty minutes in the bathroom beforehand, holding it up to the light and peering at it through a magnifying glass, looking for pinholes. You fill it with water. This takes another twenty minutes, because you're not really sure how long it would take water to trickle through a pinhole that isn't visible to the naked eye or your cheap magnifying glass. Once you've waited what seems long enough and nothing does appear to be coming through, you empty it, pat it dry, and fill it again. Just to be sure.

The first few times you used your diaphragm, your beloved came to the door of the bathroom, tortured by concern.

'Is it me?' he wanted to know. 'Are you afraid to tell me that you don't find me attractive? Was I too quick last time? Is that it, honey? Or is it because I don't work out? You hate my body, that's it, isn't it? You wish I looked more like Tom Sellick. It wouldn't bother you if Tom Sellick fell asleep while you were still talking to him. Hair! That's what's wrong. You like men with hair on their chests. Maybe if I kept my shirt on, then you wouldn't notice . . .'

After the first few times, however, he takes a book to bed with him or watches TV. Sometimes, by the time you emerge from the bathroom, he's sound asleep. Most times, in fact. Because the other thing your friends didn't tell you was how tricky inserting a diaphragm covered in spermicide can be. It slips. It slides. It jumps from your fingers and flings itself across the room. If you don't keep the toilet lid down, it'll fling itself into that as well. And then you finally get it in and your anxiety begins. When the nurse showed you how to put it in you were very confident when it came to being sure whether or not it was covering the cervix. There you were, in her bright, efficient-looking office, being watched by her bright, efficient self.

'Cervix?' you laughed. 'Of course I know where it is. Of course I can feel it.'

Somehow, though, by the time you are squatting on the bathroom floor at one in the morning with a goppy diaphragm in your hand, this confidence has been replaced by uncertainty. Is it in right? Or isn't it? Is that my cervix? *What* is a cervix? Did I put enough gop on the diaphragm? Did I put too much? Can you put it in backwards? Upside down?

The only reason you ever leave the bathroom, of course, is because you eventually realize that it doesn't matter if it's in upside down and backwards and nowhere near your cervix. Having bounced around the room for fifteen minutes, it's probably full of so many invisible holes you could use it as a sieve.

Episode Three – The Scare

He says, 'What's the matter, love? You seem a little edgy tonight.'
She says, 'Me?'
He looks around the room. As he suspected, they're all alone.

'Yes,' he says, 'you. You hardly ate any dinner and you've barely listened to a word I've been saying. What's wrong?'

She smiles, much as Joan of Arc might have smiled as she was led to the stake. 'Nothing,' she says. 'I guess I'm just a little tired.'

Later he says, 'Sweetheart, are you sure there's nothing wrong?'

She wipes the tears from her eyes with the back of her sleeve. 'No, really,' she sniffles, 'it's nothing.'

It's nothing? He looks up. 'What is it, darling?' he asks in concern. 'You know I'm here for you. Whatever it is, there's nothing you can't tell me.'

She fixes him with a moist but cold eye. 'If you were really here for me, I wouldn't have to tell you,' she says. 'You'd know.'

'I would?' He starts racking his brains. She's obviously angry with him for something – but what? Is it her birthday? Their anniversary? The anniversary of the day her dog died? Valentine's Day? The day he promised to take her out for dinner? Was she wearing something new when he came in that he failed to compliment her on? Has she changed her hair colour again? Has she lost weight? Does she look older today than she did yesterday? Mentally, he cringes. Please, he silently begs, don't let her have discovered another line or grey hair.

'I'm late!' she wails, while he's still thinking. 'Two days!'

His blood pressure drops in relief: she hasn't found another line. 'Again?' he asks.

But she doesn't hear him. She's weeping in earnest now. 'And I didn't have a chance to get one of those pregnancy kits at lunch, and then I thought I felt it coming on, and then I got home and it hadn't come on, and I was too embarrassed to go to the chemist's at the corner because I've been in there for one every month for the last six months and I'm sure that girl is laughing at me, and I know we're in no financial position to have children yet, but I don't know if I could face an abortion, though of course I'd hate to have a baby and then find out I'm as bad a mother as my mother was, and anyway we're still young, there are other things we should be doing before we tie ourselves down, but what if I had an abortion and then I couldn't have another child, that happened to one of Molly Pickering's sisters . . .'

'Darling,' he says, as he has said before, 'Sweetheart, look, let's not get all in a panic, all right? Let's think this through logically.'

She gulps for air and nods. 'You're right,' she says, 'you're absolutely right. Two days is nothing. It could be because I'm tired.

Or because of that cold I had at the beginning of the week. Or all the stress at work. Or that pizza we had the other night, it really was too oily . . .'

'Or because you're so nervous about getting pregnant,' he suggests.

'Well, yes,' she says, 'there's that too. The constant fear, the endless pressure, and my mother always asking me when we're going to have a family . . .'

'Logic,' he says. He holds up one finger. 'First of all,' he logics, 'you always wear your diaphragm, right?'

'What are you suggesting? That I deliberately tried to get pregnant?'

'Of course I'm not suggesting that. I'm trying to show you that you can't be pregnant, because you always use birth control.'

'Accidents do happen,' she says.

A great dead fish, fresh from the ice pack, finds its way into his heart. For some reason, each time he hears this piece of information it is as though he's never heard it before. 'You *do* always use birth control, don't you?' he asks in a faraway voice.

'Of course I do,' she snaps. 'What do you think I am, stupid or something? If you're so worried about it, you could use something too, you know, it doesn't all have to be up to me.'

'So,' he says, continuing his logicking, 'you've been protected every time we've made love.'

'Yes,' she says. 'Every time.'

'So you can't be pregnant.'

'No, of course I can't.' She snuffles. 'As long as nothing went wrong.'

'What could go wrong?' he asks.

'Well,' she says, 'you remember I told you about Molly Pickering's sister . . . ?'

Bed – A Retreat

Some people really hate to get out of bed.

Most people don't like to get out of bed, especially if it's a cold morning and they've been having a nice dream and it's all warm and snuggly under the duvet and outside they can hear the rain, but they do it anyway. Getting out of bed when the alarm goes off is a part of being a mature and well-balanced person.

Some people, however, don't do it anyway. They do it only under duress and, unless watched, they are likely to sneak back there at any time during the day. Where another person might rush into the kitchen and consume two family-size bags of crisps during a crisis, some people dive under the duvet at the slightest upset.

My sister, Charlotte, for instance, is a bed person.

Even when she was little, my sister Charlotte hated to get out of bed. My mother would start calling her an hour and a half before she woke the rest of us. She'd shake her gently. She'd call softly, 'Charlotte, Charlotte, love, it's time to get up.'

Charlotte would grunt. Or she would talk in her sleep. 'I'm awake,' she'd say. 'I'll get up in a minute.' That minute and several others would pass. My mother would shake Charlotte a little less gently. She would pull the covers off her. She would roll her out of the bed. 'I'm awake,' Charlotte would say. 'I'll get up in a minute.' More minutes joined the first thirty.

My mother would start dragging Charlotte out of the room by her feet. Once they reached the hall, my mother would scream, 'Get up, Charlotte! You're going to be late for school again!'

'I'm awake,' Charlotte would say.

'Your eyes aren't opened,' my mother would reply, getting a little annoyed.

'I'm awake with them closed,' Charlotte would say.

Over the years, my mother perfected a variety of techniques for this, the crucial last half hour.

Sometimes she'd lie. 'Charlotte,' she'd say, 'it's Christmas morning. Don't you want to get up and see your presents?'

Sometimes she'd threaten. 'If you don't get up right this minute, we're putting you in an orphanage and that's final.'

Once she made all of us put our coats on over our pyjamas, pick up an empty suitcase and stand in front of Charlotte (sleeping quite comfortably outside the door to the bathroom). 'Charlotte,' ordered my mother, 'Charlotte, I want you to open your eyes just for a minute. I want you to see that your sisters, your father and I are all on our way to Disneyland without you. If you want to come, you have to get up and dressed in five minutes.'

'I'm awake,' said Charlotte. 'I'll get up in a minute.'

My mother marched smartly into the bathroom, filled the laundry pail with warm water (she was never cruel) and dumped it over her youngest child.

'I'm awake,' said Charlotte. 'I'll get up in a minute.'

Funnily enough, once she moved away from home and didn't have my mother around to spend hours every morning trying to get her up, Charlotte never had any trouble waking to the alarm. You'd have thought she would be one of those people who would turn the alarm off and go right back to sleep. Or who would have to set the clock an hour early so that after she went back to sleep there was still a chance that she would wake up on time. Or who would get up in her sleep, take the alarm clock and put it somewhere where she couldn't hear it (the refrigerator or the toilet bowl, for instance, are very popular for this sort of thing). But no. The alarm would go brnng brnng brnng, and Charlotte would groan, open one eye, and get out of bed. She was never late in the mornings again. My mother, however, still wakes at five, thinking of ways to get Charlotte out of bed.

Other people find it easy enough to get out of bed, but they don't like to stay there. We call these people bedoholics. Bedoholics have been around for centuries (the Victorian middle class, in fact, made something of an art form of bedoholism). The minute anything unsettling happens, the bedoholic heads straight for the duvet. The bill arrives for the work on the roof, and instead of stomping around the flat for a few hours, cursing, screaming, muttering about debtors' prison and occasionally sobbing, like a normal person would do, the bedoholic goes to bed. The notice comes from the tax inspector with the information that they have decided to reassess 1982–83, and instead of fainting or getting drunk or calling her mother and blaming her like any emotionally stable person would do, the bedoholic goes to bed. I have one friend – a bedoholic since puberty, when he discovered that it was easier to stay in bed than venture into a hostile world with terminal acne and a tendency for breaking things – who once spent the entire month of February in bed.

'You can never be too careful about February,' he said. 'They made it short because it's usually so awful.'

Another bedoholic I know once had a party while she was in bed. The trauma of preparing a party for 100 people and then having to face them all and make sure no one passed out in the loo or was sick on the furniture proved too much for her. Thirty-eight minutes before the first guest arrived, muttering something about not having enough carrot sticks, she went to bed. She took with her a glass of wine, a bag of crisps and a book. Throughout the evening, her friends would drop in on her and chat for a while – you know, tell her who was fighting with who, or who was trying to belly dance to 'Strawberry Fields', that sort of thing, maybe bringing her another glass of wine or a few sausage rolls as well. 'It was the best party I've ever had,' she said later. Everyone else thought it was the best party she'd ever had, too, because she wasn't following her guests around the room asking them if the dip was all right and whether or not they were enjoying themselves.

Celebrity

When you're not rich and famous, you think that the one thing that would make you really happy would to be rich and famous. To have your photograph in newspapers and magazines. To see your name in the gossip columns. To appear on late-night talk shows and talk about your pets. To have people follow you down the street, or come up to you in restaurants, asking for your autograph. It would not just make you happy. It would make you ecstatic, delirious, over-the-moon!

It would also make you incredibly neurotic.

Think about how neurotic you are now, and imagine how much more neurotic it would make you if there were fifty twelve-year-olds standing in front of your house every day of the week, waiting for you to walk past a window so they could start screaming.

Think about how neurotic you are now, and just try to picture how much more neurotic you would be if you knew that people believed everything they read about you in the tabloids. Every single thing. That there were people going through your dustbins to discover the intimate secrets of your life. That you couldn't throw a chocolate wrapper away without worrying that when you opened the morning paper the headline would read: Rock Idol Axeminster Wittgenstein Addicted to Mars Bars.

Think about the paranoid terror that winds itself around your solar plexus whenever you have to walk into a crowded room where you don't know anyone, and think how paranoid you would become if every time you walked into the corner shop for a container of milk every eye in the place followed you as you went to the refrigerator case, took out a low-fat milk, carried it to the register and removed your wallet from your pocket.

Think how crazy it makes you when a friend you haven't seen or spoken to for a few weeks says, 'So, I hear you've dyed your hair again.' Some best friend Suzette is, you think, she can't keep her big mouth shut for one second. Am I on television or something? Do I have no secrets? No privacy? Can't I even dye my hair without the whole world finding out? How enraged you become when mere acquaintances accost you at parties and ask, 'Is it true that Melissa left you for a female automechanic?' Good Lord! you shout to yourself, is nothing sacred? Can't I even have a broken heart by myself? And then think how crazy and insane it would make you if you did have no secrets, no privacy, if every time you went out on a date or yelled at your beloved the whole world knew about it.

I rest my case.

THE PERILS OF THE
MODERN WORLD

Advertising

Lord knows what people did to keep their stress levels healthy before advertising became the most dominant force in our lives. In those days, all we really had to worry about was life (would we be able to continue it into tomorrow?) and death (was it going to come sooner than expected?). But not anymore, advertising has seen to that. The Wrath of God is nothing compared to the Tyranny of the Television Commercial.

Now we have to worry about how white our clothes are, how spotless our dishes, whether we're drinking the right soft drink, driving the right car, or eating the right chocolate. What's being struck by lightning or starving during a heavy winter next to not being sure if your deodorant's working? It's no wonder insecurity and indecision thrive.

You're sitting in front of the telly one night, nibbling on a biscuit and sipping a cup of tea. You're feeling pretty good about yourself. Your boss hasn't yelled at you for a week or two. The bank hasn't recalled your credit card yet. That ache in your left shin's been pretty quiet lately. Yes, on the whole, things aren't going badly, not badly at all.

And then the gunfight on the small screen stops and the commercial comes on. It's an ad for a universally popular soft drink. In a series of scenes taken from everyday life – children playing, couples washing their cars, husbands helping their wives clean out the attic, lovers kissing over a bottle of cola – the commercial builds up an image of astounding happiness and love.

You glance down at your tea. There's a greyish film floating on the top of it. You glance back at the screen. Everyone in the advertisement is attractive and full of well-being. You glance down again. There are biscuit crumbs on your lap. You are not particularly attractive. You are not full of well-being. Let's face it, you've had your moments, but on the whole you have never looked as happy or loved as these ordinary, everyday folk in the commercial. If you sprayed your wife with the hose while washing the car she'd make you sleep in the garden shed for a week. Your children can't play together for more than two seconds without trying to murder one another.

You stop feeling pretty good about yourself. Suddenly you realize just how empty and unsatisfying your life really is. Is it any wonder then, that instead of jumping to your feet and shouting, 'Who are these people? What planet do they live on?', you start sliding down in your chair? That you start asking yourself what you've done wrong. 'What have I done wrong?' you cry aloud. 'Why isn't my life full of sweetness and light?' You hang your head. 'It's my fault,' you moan. 'All my fault. It must be.' Inadequacy goose-steps into your heart. A sense of failure moves into your brain and starts unpacking. One minute ago you were perfectly O K, enjoying a few bourbon creams and a little harmless visual violence, and now you're paralysed by anxiety.

But you, of course, don't consciously realize that you're paralysed by anxiety. You think you're thirsty.

Death Is the Absence of Stress

If you take comfort from the above, or own the T-shirt, you need to relax a little more.

Shopping: Buying a Gift

No matter how much you try to avoid it, there comes a time (or several thousand times) in the life of every person when he or she has to buy a present for someone else. And unlike most things, gift buying does not become easier with practice. No matter how many Christmases, birthdays, weddings or anniversaries you successfully negotiate, each time another one comes around it is as though you have never bought a present before in your life.

You begin with purpose and enthusiasm. 'A Christmas present for Caroline,' you announce to yourself at the entrance to the shopping centre. 'That shouldn't be too hard.' You look around. There are fifty-eight shops located on three different levels. At least eighty per cent of them sell clothing of one sort or another. 'That's it!' you exclaim. 'I'll get her something to wear!'

But what? How about socks! Everyone wears socks.

You start looking at socks. You see some very nice socks. Four pairs of very nice socks that Caroline would love. But which one would she love more? The black and gold or the blue polka dots, the red and white striped or the plaid? You stand at the sock counter for twenty-seven minutes, trying to remember every article of clothing Caroline owns. You can't decide if she has anything that would go with any of these socks. Maybe not socks, you finally decide. Maybe something else.

You go to the next shop on level one. It specializes in scarves. 'Of course!' you cry, startling several shoppers trying to push their way past you. 'A scarf! Caroline would love a scarf.'

Which scarf would Caroline love? There are approximately 250 different scarves in this shop. Some are cotton, some are wool, some are silk. Some are solid colours, some are intricate patterns and designs. It takes you close to an hour, but you finally pick a lovely blue and purple scarf with silver threads running through it. You are in the queue to pay when a sobering thought hits you. *Doesn't Caroline already have a scarf like this?* You don't know. It seems so familiar, this scarf. You close your eyes. You think you can picture Caroline wearing this scarf. You concentrate. No, no, you can't picture her wearing a scarf at all. You think you remember her saying that she hates scarves. You dash from the checkout just as the cashier is saying, 'Next, please,' and you put the scarf back. You run from the store.

Several hours later, muttering to yourself, you stagger off the escalator and on to level two. You have decided to get Caroline a jumper. You almost got her a blouse on three separate occasions in three separate shops, but you became nervous about collars, and then you became nervous about sleeves, and then you became insecure about size. Jumpers, however, are jumpers. They have necks and sleeves and they aren't as size-specific as blouses. You buy yourself a very nice blue jumper and a hand-knitted one with a cow jumping over the moon. But you don't buy a jumper for Caroline. Because you suddenly remember what you gave Caroline last Christmas. A jumper. A jumper you have never seen her wear.

You limp into the coffee shop to rally your troops, staggering under the dozens of carrier bags you are carrying. Besides the two jumpers, you have bought yourself several pairs of socks, a jacket on sale, a dress that will be perfect if anyone invites you out on New Year's Eve (which probably they won't, of course, but if they did you wouldn't have to go shopping again at the last minute), and an electric carrot grater that was an absolute bargain.

You decide against buying Caroline anything to wear. It's much too time-consuming, not to mention becoming pretty expensive. If you don't get out of here soon you will not only have to spend the night, you will probably have to live here as you won't be able to pay your rent for the next twelve years.

How about a book? She has books. Notepaper? Caroline always gives you notepaper. A teapot? She has a teapot, too. Maybe a plant. Plants are always a welcome present, aren't they? You have been in Caroline's home at least forty-eight times in the last year but you can't remember ever seeing a plant. Does that mean she would love to receive one? Or does it mean that she loathes plants? The woman at the next table leans over. 'It's hell, isn't it?' she asks sympathetically. 'How about a purse?' You look a little surprised. You didn't realize you were talking out loud. 'A woman can never have too many purses,' says your new friend. After six hours in the shopping centre, that statement sounds pretty profound. 'You're right!' you exclaim. 'I'll get her a purse.'

On level three you finally locate Bag Land. Next to the array of bags, satchels, and knapsacks that hang all over the store in vari-coloured abundance, a purse seems pretty insignificant and mingey. You start looking through the bags. That bright pink one? Something more conservative? That canvas satchel would come in handy on short trips. But that two-toned nylon weekender's on special offer. You buy yourself the weekender.

On Christmas Eve you buy Caroline a pair of silver earrings from a street stall. It will be another two years before you realize that Caroline's ears aren't pierced.

Money

The office Christmas dinner is coming to a close. Everyone but Eloise, who never drinks anything stronger than straight fruit juice, and Brendan, who isn't here, is feeling mighty jolly. They are all wearing paper hats and have streamers around their necks and cracker prizes stuffed in their pockets, Richard starts telling the joke about a reindeer and a pair of tights that he tells every year, and that he has told twice this year already, and everybody is in such a good mood that no one pretends to throw up behind his back, as they usually do.

The bill comes.

Janet takes charge. 'That's fifteen into £285.41,' says Janet. She whips out her calculator. 'That's nineteen pounds and three pence, each, not including the tip,' she announces.

'It's not fifteen,' says Richard.

'What?' asks Janet.

'Brendan's not here,' says Bob. 'So it's fourteen.'

'Fourteen,' says Richard. He chuckles. 'Just like the reindeer.'

'£19.03 for a plate of pasta and half an avocado?' asks Donald. 'That seems a bit steep.'

'You had your choice between the pasta and the chicken,' Janet reminds him. 'It was up to you.'

'Some choice,' says Donald.

Richard claps a hand on Donald's shoulder. 'Look, if you don't want to pay –'

Donald pushes him off. 'I didn't say I wasn't going to pay,' he says, a little loudly. 'I just said I thought it was a bit steep.'

'I don't know what you're complaining about,' says Eloise. 'You must have had two bottles of wine by yourself.' She snatches the bill from Janet's hand. 'Just let me look at that a minute,' she says. 'I had a glass of orange juice and a glass of ice water. I'm not paying for everyone else's alcohol.'

'Oh, come on, everybody,' says Sandra. 'It's Christmas. Let's not fuss about who ate what and who drank how much.'

'I'd expect you to say that,' says Eloise. 'Not only did you have a brandy with your coffee, but your husband must make at least £60,000 a year. Why should you worry about who ate what? You're not a single mother with two children to support on a scullery maid's salary.'

'Well, if we're not going to split it evenly,' says Simon. 'I had one glass of wine and I didn't have a starter.'

'But you had two coffees, the chicken and an extra side salad,' says Eloise. 'Let's not forget that.'

'I don't know why you're getting cross with me,' says Simon. 'I'm on your side.'

Richard thumps on the table with someone's shoe. 'Look, folks,' he says, his paper hat sliding dangerously over one eye, 'if anyone feels that they shouldn't have to pay as much as everyone else, pay what you want and I'll make up the difference.'

'That's a dig at me, isn't it?' shouts Bob. He pushes back his chair. 'Because I borrowed that five pounds from you last Christmas and never paid it back.'

'What five pounds?' asks Richard. 'I forgot all about it.'

'Oh sure you did,' screams Bob. 'You forgot about it so much that you waited a whole year so you could humiliate me publicly about it.'

'I don't know how much wine I had,' says Anthea, 'but I didn't have a main course at all, I just had a starter because of my diet.'

'Look,' says Janet, 'the new amount is twenty pounds and seventeen pence.'

'It's gone up!' chorus several celebrants.

'Well, of course it has,' says Janet. 'Because Brendan's not here.'

'Well where is he?' asks Andrew. 'He does this every year, the cheap bastard. Have you ever noticed how he's never around whenever there's a collection for someone's birthday either?'

'£9.95,' says Eloise, slapping ten pounds on the table in front of Janet. 'That's what I reckon mine comes to.'

'Do you want the change?' asks Simon.

'No,' says Eloise, though not to Simon but to Janet. 'You can put it towards the gratuity. But don't think I'm giving any more than that,' she adds. 'I thought the service was appalling.'

'£20.17 each,' Janet repeats. She starts counting the money she's collected. 'We're forty pounds short,' she announces.

'Count it again,' say the men.

She counts it again.

Then Bob counts it.

Richard puts in another ten pounds and seventeen pence for Eloise.

Don counts. They're still forty pounds short.

The men order another bottle of wine. Several of the women burst into tears.

Instructions

Anyone who has even the slightest doubt that out there, beyond his front door, is a world of people who make the Mad Hatter look pretty reasonable doesn't have to go too far for proof.

Pick up the milk container. What does it say? Open Here. Open Other End. Pull back. Push. Each of us must, in a lifetime, open at least 8,000 containers of milk. At a conservative estimate. And yet the milk manufacturers feel it is necessary to provide us with detailed instructions. Why? Because if they didn't no one would ever drink any milk, that's why. We'd all be eating dry cereal and taking our coffee black. Because no matter how many times you open a container of milk, you read the instructions.

Look at the bag the dry cleaning comes back in. What does it say? It tells you not to put the bag over your head. It tells you not to get into the bag. It tells you to keep the bag out of the reach of children. Why? Because if it didn't tell us these things, a large proportion of us, removing our jacket from the plastic bag, would immediately put it over our heads. Or climb into it. Or give it to the first child we came across.

Stroll over to the freezer. Take out the frozen lasagne. Read the directions for baking the frozen lasagne. What do they say? They say: Preheat oven. Remove from box. If the purveyors of frozen lasagne feel it is necessary to instruct us that you have to take the lasagne out of the box before you put it in the oven, it can only be because they have had a lot of complaints from irate customers whose lasagne boxes caught on fire when they put them in the oven.

Sellotapephobia and Clingfilmphobia – fear of Sellotape and/or clingfilm

Having one of these phobias does not mean that you will automatically have the other; but most of us do have at least one.

'But these fears are totally justifiable,' you argue. 'Clingfilm always clings to the things you don't want it to cling to, and the Sellotape will never come off the roll. Or will come off the roll, but it'll get stuck in your hair or wind itself around your leg.'

And planes do fall out of the sky and spiders do walk up your nostrils. All fears have some basis in reality – e.g., it may not be probable that if you decide to take your life savings and go to some tropical island for a holiday there will be a revolution there on the day you arrive, you'll be held hostage in a third-class hotel, and it'll rain for the entire two weeks – but it's possible.

What we're talking about here is degree. It's one thing to worry about clingfilm. 'Oh my goodness,' you fret, 'I have to wrap the cheese up in clingfilm. The clingfilm's going to fold itself over as soon as I tear it from the roll. Then I'm going to spend fifteen minutes trying to flatten it out again. Every time I get one corner down, another will bunch up. I'll hold one end in my teeth, and then I'll slowly try to unwind the other end. But it won't work. So I'll try holding one end down with the food processor while I gently unwind the other end. It'll bunch up even tighter. Eventually, I'll be left with a small plastic ball. I'll throw it away and start again. Several hours later, when I finally have a piece of clingfilm that could be more or less used to cover the cheese, I will discover that the dog ate the cheese two hours ago and is farting in the corner.'

But it's another thing to sit down and eat a pound and a half of farmhouse cheddar in one go because you can't face the thought of trying to wrap it in clingfilm.

Flying

Up to our necks in the twentieth century as we are, it is obviously uncool to admit that you don't like planes. It's like saying you don't like indoor plumbing or running water. 'What? Are you mad?' everyone wants to know. 'You want to piss in the woods? You want to *walk* to Bombay?'

But if the truth be told, there are far more people who are afraid of flying than there are people who aren't. Which, of course, is totally reasonable. Only a few short years ago we weren't the sophisticated technocrats we are today but nervous bumpkins who didn't want to travel too close to the horizon for fear of falling off. We may now take things like microwave ovens and intergalactic travel for granted, but deep in our hearts the bumpkin still lives. And the bumpkin knows that the fact that we never evolved wings was not a divine oversight.

We were never meant to have any. We were never meant to fly around in the clouds eating imitation food and knocking back the gin, we were meant to be safe at home with our feet on the ground. What is surprising (and possibly neurotic) is that we pretend that air travel is perfectly normal.

The question is: How close to the surface is the bumpkin in you – and how close to the surface would he really like to stay?

Aeroplanes – The Quiz

Select the answer that best describes your feelings or behaviour.

1. In the scene in *Rain Man* where Raymond refuses to take a plane back to California with his brother and instead starts reeling off crash statistics, you:
   a. Laughed and sympathized with the brother.
   b. Laughed but sympathized with Raymond.
   c. Did not laugh.
   d. Started correcting his statistics.

2. What do you do after booking your flight?
   a. Finish what you were doing before you phoned the travel agent.
   b. Call your lawyer to revise your will.
   c. Call your best friend to tell her that she can wait till you come back before she returns that drill she borrowed from you in 1981.
   d. Pour yourself a drink – and then call your mother to tell her that you didn't really mean what you said about her cooking.

3. Which of the following reasons would you feel was sufficient for cancelling an air trip?
   a. Severe weather conditions, e.g., a tornado or a blizzard so bad that the airport is shut down and you can't get the car out of the drive.
   b. It's raining and you have a bit of a headache.
   c. You can't find your lucky shark's tooth.
   d. You just realized that your flight is on a Wednesday. You

never travel on Wednesdays, Fridays or any country's
national holidays – not even Romania's.
e. Even if by cancelling you lost your fare?

4. You have to go to Helsinki for an important convention. You
have to fly to Helsinki. Somehow, you have never flown before.
Even the time you went to India you went by motorbike (you
saw so much more that way). It's not that you don't think air
travel is safer than riding in a car. You think that it probably is.
You're sure the pilots, air controllers, navigators and co-pilots
are all sane, sober people who know their jobs and do them
well, despite what everyone says. Still, as your day of departure
draws nearer your anxiety level starts to rise. You start looking
for omens. If the phone bill is low, that means you'll never see
sunset in Helsinki. If you really are going bald, then you'll not
only see sunset in Helsinki, you'll probably be back for
Christmas. You even find yourself hoping that if there is going
to be a major air disaster it happens before your flight, thus
dramatically increasing your chances of arriving without
incident. In the end, you:
a. Take a stiff whisky or a couple of tranquillizers and sleep
   through lunch.
b. Take a stiff whisky, a couple of tranquillizers, and spend the
   entire flight pointing out structural weaknesses in the wing to
   your seatmates.
c. Have to be knocked out and carried on board. You sit next
   to a three-year-old boy who is also in the stewardess's
   charge.
d. Get on the plane, sit in your seat, look around and decide
   that everyone else on board looks like characters in a disaster
   movie, and bolt for the door.

5. As we all know, before the airlines will let you have a drink they
make you sit through a presentation of safety precautions: How
to use the oxygen mask; How to leave the plane in a calm and
orderly manner; How to inflate your life vest, turn your little
light on and blow your little whistle; How to conduct yourself
while bobbing around in the storm-tossed ocean. Many people
(the people who will inflate their life vests *before* they leave the
plane, who will yank their oxygen masks out of place and then

commandeer yours, who will forget where the emergency exits are and cause a jam, who will make the ocean seem very small) take this as an opportunity for a quick nap before dinner. You:

a. Half-listen, half-wonder if they're going to remember that you ordered a macrobiotic meal (you are not a vegan, but you've heard that the food they give vegetarians is significantly better than the food they give carnivores).

b. Not only pay proper attention, but read through the emergency instructions as well.

c. Take notes.

d. Start to cry.

6. The night before your trip begins you:

a. Spend a quiet evening with your loved ones, just as you would have done were you not planning to defy gravity the following morning.

b. Pack. Probably several times.

c. Run up your credit card to its limit. That way, should something happen, not, of course, that it will, you will at least have the last laugh.

d. Decide to pack in the morning and get drunk instead. Having a hangover will give you something other than death to worry about.

Give yourself one point for every a., two for every b., three for every c., four for every d., and twenty-five for every e. If you scored six points – which no one could – you are so unneurotic that it must sometimes occur to you that you're on the wrong planet. Anything above six is normal.

Appliancephobia – fear of appliances

Some people are, of course, afraid of all appliances, but most people with this particular phobia are only afraid of their own appliances. They think their appliances hate them. They believe that at night, while they sleep, their toaster and their blender and their VCR get together and discuss the best way of ruining their life. They can't be convinced that the time the food processor ate that tie, or the incident involving the belching Hoover and the exploding light bulb weren't deliberately planned by the appliance in question. The number of people afraid of answering machines alone is at the level of an epidemic.

Answering Machines

Like the telephone itself, the answering machine was basically a good idea. Helpful. Utilitarian. Practical. Sensible. Something to bring peace of mind to the troubled voyager in this chaotic and maddening world.

Hey, you think, that is a good idea. And so you buy an answering machine. Having bought an answering machine, you have to put a message on it. But what message? If you say, 'Hi, this is Daniel, there's no one here to take your call' you are making a public announcement that your home and stereo system are unguarded for an indefinite period. If you say, 'Hi, this is Melanie, I'm busy right now', you are notifying every heavybreather and damaged personality in the world that you are a single woman living alone. If you use someone else's voice or a piece of music you will have to give your number, so that your friends will know that they reached you and not someone else. You don't want to give your number, however, because if the person who phoned is a damaged personality who got you by mistake they will then be able to phone you again. The answering machine sits in its box in the hallway for three months while you decide what message you should use. Finally, bruised friends who have been tripping over it regularly force you to plug it in. 'Wait till you see,' they tell you. 'It's going to change your life.'

And it does change your life. Before, if you were away for an evening or a weekend or even a week or two you would come home to your empty flat with a feeling of joy. It's good to be home, you'd think. You'd kick off your shoes and make yourself a cup of tea and think of all the people who were trying to get you while you were out. Hundreds of people. Wonderful people. All of them wanting to talk to you. All of them wondering where you are, imagining you out having a fantastic time.

But once you become the owner of an answering machine, all illusions as to your own popularity are shattered once and for all. You come home from a week out of town. You drop your bags and rush to the answering machine. The red light is steady. 'But that's impossible,' you cry out loud. 'I've been gone seven days! Someone must have called.' There must be something wrong. Perhaps the tape is so full that the machine has shut itself off. You push playback. The tape isn't full. There is nothing on the tape, except part of a message from your mother from four weeks before. You shake the machine. You hit it. The machine must be broken. To test if the machine is broken or not, you run out of the house, into the blizzard, and around the corner to a callbox. You phone yourself. You answer. 'We're all very busy at the moment,' you say, 'please leave a message after the tone and someone will get back to you as soon as possible.' 'It's me!' you shout. 'Just testing!' You race back home and to your machine. The little light is blinking. You push playback. 'It's me!' you shout. 'Just testing!'

And once you become the owner of an answering machine you realize something else. Your friends don't want to talk to you. That's why they all have answering machines. They have answering machines so that they can screen calls before they find themselves talking to someone they don't want to talk to. Someone they find boring. Someone who might invite them to a mediocre dinner of boiled spaghetti if they don't have time to think of a reason for not going first. They have answering machines so that they don't have to talk to you. There you are, stammering, 'Hello, Toby and Carla, I just called up for a little chat, and to see if you wanted to come to dinner on Thursday,' and they're sitting there the whole time, laughing and congratulating themselves on being clever enough not to answer the phone before they were sure who it was.

'Gosh,' you're saying right about now. 'I suppose answering machines don't make life very stress-free after all, do they?'

We haven't scratched the surface yet.

You are supposed to go to dinner at the home of a friend from work whom you don't know very well. On your way to dinner you become inexplicably lost. You are halfway to the airport before you realize you shouldn't be going to the airport. You make an illegal U-turn across a dual carriageway and head back in the direction you were coming from. You not only have no idea where your would-be hosts live, you have no idea where you are. You drive for forty-five minutes, talking to yourself the whole time, and periodically bursting into tears. At last you see a phone booth. You pull over, causing the gentleman behind you to call you several unpleasant names and throw an empty plastic cup at your bumper. You race to the phone. You put in your coin. The phone rings. The phone is answered. But not by your friend. Not by anyone or anything even remotely human. At number 411 1114 there is a buzz, a hum, and something that sounds like Cab Calloway singing 'There Ain't Nobody Here but Us Chickens' in a bad storm. At what you take to be the sound of the tone, you say, 'Um . . . uh . . . ah . . . well . . . um . . . Henry?' and slam down the receiver.

Many people, confronted unexpectedly with an answering machine, react in exactly that way. They panic. They were all set to chat happily for the next three hours, but the sound of a self-conscious, 'Hi, this is Harry, I'm mountain climbing in the Himalayas at the moment, but if you leave a message I'll get right back to you,' or some indecipherable piece of music that may or may not represent Harry, makes their minds go blank. They're lucky if they can remember who they are, let alone why they were calling.

And just the other day I had a phonecall from an old boyfriend of mine. I hadn't heard from him in three years, not since the night I woke up at three in the morning to find him putting on his clothes. 'Where are you going?' I asked. 'I'm going to get something to eat,' he replied. Anyway, as I said, it had been thirty-five months, four days and sixteen hours since we'd last spoken. Despite the fact that I'd been not angry, exactly, but pretty upset the last time we had talked, my heart did a little flip flop at the sound of his voice. Was he coming back after all? I wondered. Had he really gone out for fish and chips and then been too shy to return? Maybe he'd been in an accident coming back from getting his fish and chips and had had amnesia for the past three years. That was why I never saw him again, he had amnesia!

He wanted to know if it was I who left the hate message on his answering machine. 'Hate message?' I asked. 'Someone left a *hate* message on your answering machine?'

'Quite a long one,' he said.

It had never occurred to me that someone might leave a hate message on my answering machine. Had it occurred to you? Obscene phonecalls, yes. Heavy breathing, of course. But hate messages? My God, I thought to myself as my heart thudded to my boots. Something else to worry about!

Cash Machines

It is a Sunday morning and you are going somewhere that requires currency as opposed to cheques or credit cards. You have no money. You check through every pocket of every item of clothing that you have, you go through all the drawers and every bag, and you come up with four coins, three of them foreign. There's nothing for it, you're going to have to use the cash machine. Off you go to the cash machine. There are several people hovering around in front of it, muttering to themselves, so you go around the block a few times, waiting for them all to leave. You have more than one fear when it comes to cash machines. The first is that someone might mug you. The second is that you won't be able to work it. The third is that you will be able to work it, but it won't give you any money.

At last, there is no one around. You hurry over to the machine. It greets you in a friendly enough manner. You insert your card. Then you insert it properly. It asks you to tap in your number. You tap in your number. As you are tapping in your number, someone comes up behind you. The machine informs you that you have tapped in the wrong number.

'Heh, heh, heh,' you say out loud. 'Silly me.'

You start to tap in what you hope is the right number, but because you're a little worried that the person behind you can tell what number you're keying in, you practically climb on to the screen and start singing a little song as you do so. The machine asks you what service you'd like, and you say 'deposit'. Several more people come up behind you. You have no idea how to get out of 'deposit'.

'Oh well um,' you say out loud, 'now how did that happen?'

Eventually you get out of 'deposit' and into 'withdrawal'. You tell the machine how much money you want. But instead of giving you any money, it takes your card. You say, 'Hey!'

Behind you, several people, all of whom are glad this is happening to you and not to them, start to laugh.

'Hey,' you repeat, this time a little more loudly. 'What's going on?'

The machine remains silent. 'I'm not overdrawn!' you shout. 'My card hasn't expired. What's the deal?' In your nightmares, the machine always answers. It says, 'I don't like you!' Or, 'You're too slow.' But in real life it says nothing of the kind.

In real life, it says, 'Welcome. Please insert your card.'

Computers

Unlike people who *think* that their appliances are out to get them, people who are afraid of computers *know* that their machine has it in for them.

'This sounds a little paranoid to me,' you say.

Not at all. Computers, after all, are the machines with a brain. And anything with a brain, as we know only to well, is dangerous.

You buy a computer because everyone you know who has one, or has ever thought of having one, even if all they do is play dungeons and dragons on it, tells you how it will change your life. And it does. It's great. You can put all of your work on it. You can put the household records on it. You can make your accountant smile; no longer is she given carrier bags filled with balled-up receipts, but an annotated record on a model print out. At first you are joyous; exuberant. Everything is blissful until the day your computer eats an entire day's work. You tell it to do A., and instead it inhales seven hours of text and leaves you with one sentence: #$%@££¼+ __**&¢**%$??!

You can't believe it. 'I can't believe it!' you cry. 'This can't be happening.'

It is happening.

Thus begin your daily conversations with the troubleshooter at the computer company.

'Could be anything,' he says. 'Did you leave the disks near a magnetic field?'

Magnetic field? You have no idea what a magnetic field is. Which was, you quickly discover, a pleasant state to be in. Magnetic fields are all over the place. Anywhere there is something electric. 'But everything's electric,' you whine to the troubleshooter. 'The computer's electric for heaven's sake.'

He is unsympathetic. He warns you about heat, cold, dust, and sudden voltage surges. He warns you never to turn off in the middle of a job. 'Don't get caught in a power failure,' he jokes.

All at once you are aware of what a sensitive and even temperamental thing your computer is. And how much more there is to worry about in heaven and earth than you had previously thought. What are earthquakes, flash floods and dodgy water next to a computer that will take fifty pages of revolutionary quantum theory and turn it into a blank page with a couple of exclamation marks at the end?

Where once you commanded your computer blithely, even cavalierly, you are now timorous. And rightly so. Every time you forget how sensitive it is – and how much it clearly dislikes you – it wipes out hours of work and blinks little messages to you: Machine Busy! File Empty! Disk Closed! You Wish!

And then, one chilly afternoon, the horrible significance of it all descends on you like a ton of potatoes. The whole world is on computer now! Everything. Banks. Taxes. Health. Employment. Defence. Even the mail order computer from which you buy small, unuseful household gadgets. What if there's a national blackout? A global one? Swooshwoosh. Millions, no, billions of people, made invisible in a matter of seconds. Gone all your records! Gone all your money! Gone your order for a musical cake plate!

You buy a notebook and a fountain pen and talk to yourself even more than you used to.

Leaving-Things-Onphobia

A fear of leaving things on, locking things in, or leaving things out. The most common phobia of all – the one that all of us have to some degree or another. It's amazing that my dictionary forgot to list it. There is, in fact, probably no one who has never left the house, got halfway to where they're going, and suddenly thought to himself or herself, *Oh my God! I left the iron on! Did I leave the iron on? No, I'm sure I turned it off. No, that was yesterday I remember turning it off. What about today? I have no idea. I can't remember today.*

Leaving the House

Jamie and Denise are going away for the weekend. They stand in the sitting-room, side by side, their luggage piled before them, except for the two garment bags that are hanging on the back of the door.

'Is that everything?' asks Jamie. 'You remembered my grey trousers and an extra jumper in case it turns cold?' He consults a list in his hand.

'Darling,' says Denise, 'we checked everything off when we packed, didn't we?'

'I know we did, love,' says Jamie, 'but mistakes have been made. What about the time you checked off seven pairs of socks, and when we got to Barcelona we discovered there were only six?'

'I wasn't the one who checked off the socks,' says Denise. 'I was in charge of the first-aid kit and the toiletries.'

'I don't want to fight,' says Jamie. 'I just don't want to get to the country and find out that my grey trousers are still at home.'

'If it's checked off, darling,' says Denise, 'then they're in your garment bag.'

Jamie frowns. 'Do you think they're all right in there?' he asks. 'Maybe I should put them in the black one. It's a lot better.'

'They've been in there all night,' says Denise. 'I think they can survive the two hour trip to your mum's.'

Jamie prepares to pick up a few suitcases. 'Well, then,' he smiles, 'I suppose we're ready to leave.'

Denise puts a hand on his wrist. 'You made sure the windows are all shut, didn't you?'

Jamies's blue eyes cloud. 'I'll just check one more time, shall I?'

'I'll make sure all the lights are out while you're doing that,' Denise offers.

Jamie returns from checking the windows. 'Everything's unplugged isn't it?' he calls.

'I think so,' Denise, who can't decide whether or not she considers the illuminated dial of the clock radio a light or not, shouts back.

Jamie comes into the bedroom. 'You're leaving the radio plugged in?'

'Well, we did last time,' says Denise.

'But that was because my mother was here,' Jamie reminds her. 'My mother never unplugs anything, not even the television. It's a wonder she's lasted this long.'

'You're right,' says Denise, 'I'll unplug it.'

Jamie and Denise gather their luggage and start towards the door. 'Just one minute, sweetheart,' says Denise. 'I'd better use the loo before we go.'

When she returns Jamie decides to use the loo.

He comes back to the sitting-room to discover it empty. 'Denise!' he yells. 'Denise! Where are you?'

'I'm in the kitchen,' she yells back. 'I just wanted to make sure we hadn't left anything out. Remember how the Caradocs got mice that time they went away overnight and left out a packet of digestives by accident.'

'The tap's turned off tightly, right?' asks Jamie.

'What did you do with those crisps you were eating in the bedroom last night?' asks Denise, coming back to the sitting-room. 'You did finish them, didn't you?'

'And I threw them away,' says Jamie proudly.

'Where?'

Their eyes meet in a look of mutual horror.

'I'll just empty the wastebaskets before we go,' says Jamie quickly.

Denise goes back into the bathroom to check her make-up.

'Darling,' calls Jamie, having returned from emptying the bins, 'what are you doing?'

'I can't wear this blouse,' says Denise. 'It'll look like I've slept in it by the time we get there.'

'You're right,' says Jamie. 'My mother's so fussy. I'd better change my shirt, too.'

Denise and Jamie make it to the hallway.

'Did I lock the top lock?' he asks her as he locks the bottom.

'Yes,' says Denise.

'You're sure?'

She frowns. 'Well, I think you did.'

'But did you see me lock it?'

'Well, I thought I saw you lock it.'

Jamie sighs. He unlocks the top lock and locks it again. 'Right,' he says, 'let's hit the road.'

They make it out of the front door. Denise locks the two front door locks.

They start down the path to the street. 'You locked both locks, didn't you?' asks Jamie.

'Yes,' says Denise, 'I'm sure I did.'

'Positive?'

'Jamie,' says Denise, 'you were standing right behind me. You saw me lock them with your own two eyes. I always lock them, it's like second nature. Let's just get in the car and get on our way. If you hadn't decided to take a shower before we left, we would have been there by now.' Denise stops in the middle of the street. She looks around. She is all alone. 'Jamie!' she cries. 'Jamie! Where are you?'

Denise arrives back at their house just as Jamie is coming down the path. 'I couldn't remember if I'd locked the bottom lock or not,' he says brightly. 'And so long as I was up there, I thought I should make sure that the stove was off and the kettle was unplugged.'

'Thank God for that,' says Denise. 'Remember last time we had to turn around when we were already on the motorway because we couldn't remember if the iron was on or not?'

Denise and Jamie get in the car. 'You're sure we have everything?' asks Jamie as they strap themselves in. 'Clothes, the racquets, the book you borrowed from my mother . . .'

Denise slaps her forehead. 'Oh, no!' she wails. 'The sherry for your father. I left it in the kitchen.'

Jamie winks devilishly. 'No you didn't,' he smiles. 'I noticed it when I went back and put it in my bag.'

'And the chocolates too?' asks Denise.

'Chocolates?' echoes Jamie.

Forty-five minutes later, bombing along the motorway, Jamie turns to Denise and says, 'Darling, did you notice if I double-locked the front door or not?'

Long-Oddsphobia – fear of things that are very very unlikely to happen

It is, for instance, very unlikely that a car is going to leave the road, cross the pavement and enter the window of the restaurant where you are eating, yet there are quite a few people who can't sit down to lunch without the possibility of this happening crossing their minds. Sometimes it means that they have to move to the back of the restaurant, but then it might occur to them that something in the kitchen could explode. (What if, for instance, the rubbish has been sitting in the alley behind the kitchen for longer than it should because of a secret strike by dustmen and, therefore, the gases have built up in the rubbish? Well, what will happen is there will be one of those rare but not impossible cases of spontaneous combustion, that you hear about from time to time. The kitchen will go up and you, sitting near the kitchen because you're afraid a taxi is going to come in through the front window, will be thrown several yards by the blast, that's what if.) Or you might be afraid that someone might fall through the skylight. Or that if you leave the front door open for too long squirrels will get into the house and take it over.

Twentieth-century Angst

My Aunt Fiona has always been very much a woman of her times. In the Sixties, she spent several years on an ashram in India. In the Seventies, she was the first person in our family (and the last as far as I can remember) to discover the anti-ageing properties inherent in taking 200 vitamins a day. In the Eighties she made a fortune working the stock market. Now that the Nineties are upon us, Aunt Fiona has officially banned Halloween, *ET*, the Care Bears, oriental carpets, CND, and evolution from her home.

'She doesn't like oriental carpets? I thought everyone liked oriental carpets.'

They used to. But the times are changing again. Now, my Aunt Fiona claims, people are realizing that the road to hell is covered with oriental rugs.

'The road to hell?'

Covered with oriental rugs and crowded with CND members, funny-looking aliens, Care Bears, witches and, one presumes, the unhappy spirit of Charles Darwin.

What's happened, my Aunt Fiona says, is that the twentieth century has pushed man into the stratosphere – well, beyond the stratosphere actually – when he was still trying to learn how to walk on land. He has accepted all sorts of satanic toys as perfectly all right when in fact they're not. He's toying with damnation.

'Oriental carpets? CND?'

The Lord is obviously not the only one who works in mysterious ways.

'I don't see how you can call this twentieth-century angst, though. I mean, people worried about witches and aliens in the Dark Ages.'

But not about oriental carpets, as far as I know. What makes this a particularly twentiety-century angst is the blend of the new and the old, the ability to repeat ancient anxieties and add to them anxieties whose existence alone should disprove them – e.g., how is it possible to believe in potions made of newt eyes and bat wings when we've split the atom?

Which means, I guess, that Aunt Fiona is right. We've gone too fast. For there is one great question that has emerged in the twentieth century. This question has arisen, experts agree, because man now controls so much of his world and his environment that he finds it slightly bewildering to discover that he is still an emotional wreck, and little more, in truth, than a dust mote batted around by fate and temperamental forces that don't always seem that kind.

The question is: Why me?

The answer, of course, is: Why not?

A NOTE ON THE AUTHOR

A distinguished therapist with offices in London, New York and Gstaad, Susan F. Young is a former holder of the world high-jump record and mother of six extremely rich and nice children. She worries about everything.